Memories of Quedgeley Gloucestershire

by

Caroline Meek JP

First published in the United Kingdom in 2023

Self-Published By Kindle Direct Publishing

ISBN 9798862693904

© Caroline Meek. 2023

The Author hereby asserts her moral right to be identified as the Author of the Work.

All rights reserved. No part of this publication may be produced, stored in a retrieval system, or transmitted in any form or by any means, electronic, mechanical, photocopying, recording or otherwise, without the prior permission of the publisher and copyright holder.

British Library Cataloguing in Publication Data

A catalogue record for this book is available from the British Library

Cover Images

Top Left – Saint James Church Quedgeley

Middle Right – Gloster Meteor, Gate guard of RAF Quedgeley

Bottom Right - The Thatch Inn, Bristol Road Quedgeley

Rear – Caroline Meek (Author) & Husband Kenneth Meek

Dedication

To my Family and all my Gloucestershire friends.

Acknowledgements

I would like to acknowledge all those individuals and local organisations who produced some of the material used in this book. In particular:

- Books and notes available from past Church Rectors
- Historic Gloucester by Philip Moss
- Quedgeley Community Trust (including the Quedgeley News) (https://www.quedgeleycommunitytrust.co.uk/)
- The Gloucester Citizen (gloucestercitizen.co.uk)

More information on the events within Quedgeley mentioned within this book can be found at Gloucester Records Office.

Amongst the many people who have helped provide the content of this book and to which I give my thanks, are (in surname alphabetical order):

- Richard Cale
- Harry Meek
- Roseanna Meek
- Susan Parker
- Guy Selwyn
- Revd Geoffrey Stickland
- Jean Turner
- Andrew Wakely
- Lesley Whitaker

Every effort has been made to obtain all relevant copyright permissions. If I have missed anything I would like to hear about it. Any errors are my own and any corrections or new information would be gratefully received.

I would also like to thank Jacqueline Hall and Valerie Harris for proof-reading this book. Finally, my thanks go to Glenn Duff from Quedgeley Computer Solutions (www.quedgeley.com) for his technical help in the production of this book.

Table of Contents

Dedication i
Acknowledgements i
Table of Contents ii
Table of Figures iii
Chapter 1 – Introduction 1
Chapter 2 – Our Geography 3
Chapter 3 – Our History 13
Chapter 4 – Our Buildings 33
Chapter 5 – Our Organisations and Clubs 89
Chapter 6 – Our People 109
Appendix A – 1906 Quedgeley Parish Magazine 139
Appendix B – Church Notes by Revd H Hadow 143
Appendix C – 1861 Census (as printed) 149
Index 151

Table of Figures

Figure 1 – Hawkes' Bakery (later Jowett's Grocery) 5
Figure 2 – Quedgeley Court Lodge 5
Figure 3 – The Thatch Restaurant 6
Figure 4 – Forge Cottage 6
Figure 5 – Packers Cottage 7
Figure 6 – Another Thatched Cottage on Bristol Road (now gone) 7
Figure 7 – Sims Bridge on the Gloucester & Sharpness Canal 8
Figure 8 – The Severn Bore at Stonebench 9
Figure 9 – Surfing on The Severn Bore 10
Figure 10 – Pleasure boats on the Gloucester & Sharpness Canal 11
Figure 11 – Tall Ship on the Gloucester & Sharpness Canal 12
Figure 12 – The Plough Hotel circa 1900 15
Figure 13 – Customer outing from the Plough Hotel circa 1925 16
Figure 14 – Tea-time at the Plough Hotel circa 1932 16
Figure 15 – Another outing from the Plough Hotel circa 1950 17
Figure 16 – The Retreat Guest House 17
Figure 17 – Quedgeley Rovers AFC Team, 1925-26 season 18
Figure 18 – Quedgeley Cricketers, 1934 18
Figure 19 – A show from Marion Macloud's Dancing School 19
Figure 20 – Church fête in the First Quedgeley Village Hall, 1950 20
Figure 21 – Coronation Celebration fancy dress 21
Figure 22 – Elaine Brint and Jennifer Ely in fancy dress 21
Figure 23 – Harry Gage in the First Quedgeley Village Hall 21
Figure 24 – St James Close Notes (page 1) 22
Figure 25 – St James Close Notes (page 2) 23
Figure 26 – B.P. Miller, one of the many Petrol Tankers 24
Figure 27 – Residents and surveyor discussing the sewerage system 26
Figure 28 – The opening of the M5 link road 28
Figure 29 – Birthday and Retirement of Ursula Norman 29
Figure 30 – Manpower Services Commission lunch preparations for the elderly 30
Figure 31 – St James' Church Reredos 34
Figure 32 – St James' Church Nave and Pews 35
Figure 33 – St James' Church Pulpit and Choir Stalls 36
Figure 34 – St James' Church North Porch 37
Figure 35 – St James' Church South Porch 37
Figure 36 – St James' Church Chancel, East Window 39
Figure 37 – St James' Churchyard (ancient view) 40
Figure 38 – St James' Churchyard (modern view) 41
Figure 39 – St James' Church War Memorial 42
Figure 40 – Revd Hadow with a few of the choir 48
Figure 41 – The Rectory 49

Figure 42 – The Rectory Housemaids 49
Figure 43 – Housekeeper Lucy Meadows with husband Thomas, circa 1938 50
Figure 44 – A Play performed on The Rectory lawn 51
Figure 45 – The Rectory at the time it was sold 52
Figure 46 – My husband and I were the first private owners of The Old Rectory 52
Figure 47 – Wounded soldiers retraining at The Manor 54
Figure 48 – Woolstrop Lodge 55
Figure 49 – The Auction of Quedgeley House Estate in 1939 56
Figure 50 – Quedgeley House Estate Contents for auction in 1939 57
Figure 51 – Woolstrop Cottage on School Lane 58
Figure 52 – Woolstrop Farm 58
Figure 53 – Cary Carter from Woolstrop Farm 59
Figure 54 – Field Court Farm pre-1970 60
Figure 55 – The Munitions 'Canary Girls' 61
Figure 56 – WPC Marion Sandover 61
Figure 57 – Flight Lieutenant Robert Coventry 62
Figure 58 – Queen Mary's visit to RAF Quedgeley in 1941 63
Figure 59 – Celebrating 40 years of the RAF in Quedgeley, 1939-1979 65
Figure 60 – The closing of RAF Quedgeley: Formal Closure Lunch 66
Figure 61 – The closing of RAF Quedgeley: Band of the RAF Regiment 66
Figure 62 – The closing of RAF Quedgeley: Service of Commemoration 67
Figure 63 – The closing of RAF Quedgeley: Lowering the Ensign 68
Figure 64 – RAF Quedgeley Annual Party in 1980 69
Figure 65 – The opening of The First Quedgeley Village Hall in 1928 70
Figure 66 – The opening of The Second Quedgeley Village Hall in 1962 72
Figure 67 – The opening ceremony for the Second Quedgeley Village Hall 73
Figure 68 – The Trustees & Secretary for the Second Quedgeley Village Hall 73
Figure 69 – Old Time Dance in the Second Quedgeley Village Hall in 1968 74
Figure 70 – St James' Harvest Supper in the Second Quedgeley Village Hall, 1963 .. 74
Figure 71 – The St James Centre 75
Figure 72 – The opening of the Youth and Community Centre in 1995 76
Figure 73 – Mrs Hinder & Miss Marshall open the Youth and Community Centre .. 77
Figure 74 – The laying of the Foundation Stone for Severnvale Shopping Centre 78
Figure 75 – The Original Basket Maker Pub 79
Figure 76 – The opening of the Library in 1989 79
Figure 77 – Cutting the first turf for the Health Centre 80
Figure 78 – Beautiful hand-drawing of the Methodist Church 81
Figure 79 – Methodist Church Sunday School Outing, 1920s 81
Figure 80 – The Sunday School (on the right), taken in 1938 82
Figure 81 – Children at The National School in 1898 83
Figure 82 – The Church of England School (rear view) 83
Figure 83 – The Dedication Service of the Church of England School 84
Figure 84 – Children (Group 3) at The Church of England School (circa 1930) 85

Figure 85 – Children at the Church of England School in 1953 86
Figure 86 – Mothers' Union Annual Festival at the Cathedral in 1975 89
Figure 87 – Quedgeley W.I. Meeting during a power cut in 1970 90
Figure 88 – Quedgeley W.I. Keep Fit Session in 1983 91
Figure 89 – Quedgeley W.I. win a prize in the Annual Show in 2005 91
Figure 90 – The RAF Commanding Officer opening a Youth Club Fête 93
Figure 91 – One of the Youth Club fêtes 94
Figure 92 – Scout Trip to Luxembourg in 1958 95
Figure 93 – Cub Pack with Cub Leader Mrs Warrener 96
Figure 94 – The late Princess Margaret visiting The Rainbows 97
Figure 95 – Infant Welfare's Nurse Carpenter with Margaret Uzzell in 1965 98
Figure 96 – Infant Welfare Committee Goodbye Presentation 98
Figure 97 – The Golden Age Club knitters in 1993 99
Figure 98 – Parish Council Beating The Bounds in 1979 106
Figure 99 – The opening of the first Parish Council Office on 29 January 1993 107
Figure 100 – The expansion of new homes in Quedgeley 107
Figure 101 – Frederick Cale (1862-1949) 110
Figure 102 – Jack Cale (1901-1979) 111
Figure 103 – Jack Cale (left) with son Richard Cale 111
Figure 104 – Laura Parsons and postman Bill Compton 116
Figure 105 – Letter from The Queen Mother for taking in refugees 132
Figure 106 – Letter of gratitude from King George VI in 1946 134
Figure 107 – Useful World War II Dates Summary from King George VI 135
Figure 108 – Church Magazine (January 1906) 139
Figure 109 – Revd Hadow's Notes 143

Chapter 1 – Introduction

My story is mainly to tell you about the growth of Quedgeley over the years and the interesting people whom I have had the pleasure of knowing.

When I was born in Quedgeley in 1936, the main A38 (Leeds to Exeter) ran through the middle of the village with four lanes running off it leading to farms. The population was under 1,000. At the time of writing, the population (including Kingsway) is now around 28,000 and no working farms.

Over the years I have collected many articles on local history and current news. It was not until my husband died at the end of 2016 that I decided that it was time to downsize and I moved into a smaller home, still in Quedgeley. When I counted the number of boxes of records I had of the past, I decided to put it all together into a book. COVID-19 lockdown came and I had no excuse.

Many good books have been published over the years on the City of Gloucester and surrounding villages. I did not want to repeat the same history over again. It is so easy today to find out about the past in the Gloucester Records Office or online for example with Wikipedia.

The contents of the book are only part of my collection of memories but I hope I have mentioned some of the interesting happenings over the years.

Chapter 2 – Our Geography

Early Geography

Quedgeley is a town to the south of Gloucester in Gloucestershire, England, United Kingdom.

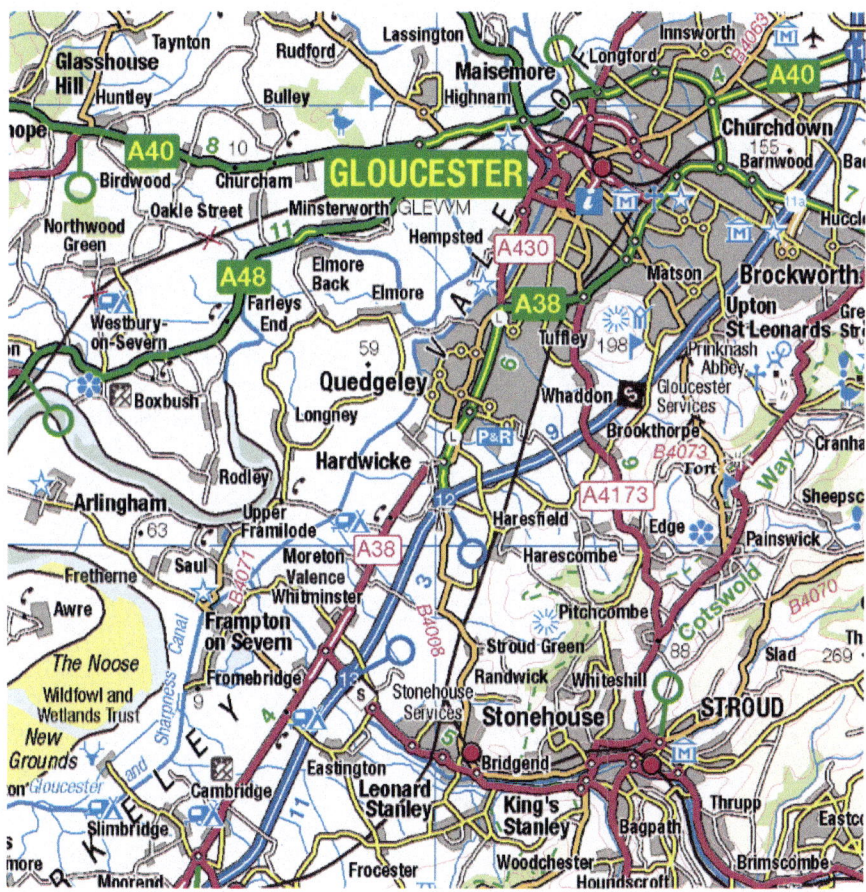

[Source: Ordnance Survey OpenData. 1:250000 Scale Colour Raster Map. Contains public sector information licensed under the Open Government Licence v3.0]

Quedgeley, found three miles south of Gloucester, has had a busy main highway running through the middle of it from the beginning of Roman times.

Quedgeley once had a triangular green of thirty-five acres which stretched from the Church, either side of the highway towards Gloucester. It was called Great Green and was still there in 1841.

Over the centuries there were many boundary changes. The Enclosure Acts of 1841 and 1866 ordered by the Government, finally sorted the land and recorded it. It was handwritten into a book, which was placed at the Gloucester Records Office. Land was set aside for recreation. A pound for stray animals was provided at The Chantry, Bristol Road. Twenty-five pensioners were given an allotment to cultivate. The Enclosure book can still be viewed.

The boundary on the west was the River Severn, together with the Dimor Brook (Now called Dimore/Fishers Brook). The east boundary was the Qued Brook and, years later, the railway line built in the mid-nineteenth century.

Quedgeley is flat and rises at its highest only to a one hundred feet contour. It is entirely on the Lower Lias and has patches of gravel. The farmers grew wheat, barley and beans. The River Severn banks provided reeds, which were used for thatching cottages. Teasels were cut to use in the cloth mills at Stroud. Fishing was one of the main sources of income. In the fifteenth century the Walsh family of Netheridge Estate owned a fishery in the Severn producing mainly salmon and eels.

Quedgeley had 1,450 acres in 1882. After many boundary changes in 1882, 1885, 1900, 1935, 1951 and 1954, Quedgeley was finally left with 1,420 acres (as of 1991).

Key Roads
Bristol Road
In 1599, it was said that the parishioners of Quedgeley failed to repair the King's highway (Bristol Road was formerly known as the Kings Way) which passed through the parish.

In 1675, in the north of the parish, the road passed over the Qued Brook by a wooden bridge. It was called Wainbridge. The highway was a turnpike from 1726 to 1877. A stone toll house was still there in the 1950s by the side of the Gloucester & Sharpness Canal, at the Gloucester City Boundary.

In 1885, the Methodist Church was built on the Bristol Road in the south. Halfway through the parish, the first Village Hall was opened by the roadside in 1928. Opposite the Village Hall was Hawkes' Bakery (later Jowett's Grocery).

Figure 1 – Hawkes' Bakery (later Jowett's Grocery)

In the late 1950s, Goodridge Avenue was built off the Bristol Road by the canal and small factories such as Daystrom (who assembled electronic instruments) and Baxter's Abattoir, brought employment. In 1958, Bristol Road in the north of Quedgeley ended at a roundabout. It joined with Cole Avenue, which was the end of Gloucester's unfinished ring road started in the 1930s. Quedgeley Court and its Lodge, built around 1880 nearby, were demolished.

Figure 2 – Quedgeley Court Lodge

In 1996, the roundabout was replaced by many sets of traffic lights. From there, traffic from Quedgeley could now join the new bypass (A38) and travel towards Hardwicke, or join the completed Gloucester Ring Road and go over the canal, through Hempsted towards Gloucester. From Cole Avenue travelling through Quedgeley, the old A38 became the new B4008 going all the way to Stonehouse.

There are four surviving properties on the east side of the Bristol Road which date back to the sixteenth century or earlier. They include The Thatch Restaurant (it no longer has a thatched roof), Forge Cottage, Packers Cottage and Manor Farm House (see page 53).

Figure 3 – The Thatch Restaurant

Figure 4 – Forge Cottage

Figure 5 – Packers Cottage

Figure 6 – Another Thatched Cottage on Bristol Road (now gone)

Sims Lane

This is found in the north of the parish, off the west side of Bristol Road. It was once called Crockens Lane in the Middle Ages. It led to the Hamlet of Woolstrop, which in 1252 paid the land tax to Dudstone Kings Barton Hundred, but by 1775 it was part of Whitstone Hundred, with the rest of Quedgeley. The Gloucester & Sharpness Canal (see page 11) cut across Sims Lane, causing great inconvenience for landowners from 1794.

In the late nineteenth century and early twentieth century small brick houses were built along Sims Lane. If you travelled to the end of the lane, you reached Sims Bridge which went over the canal and then took you to a property originally called Indian Bungalow, which later became Riversmead Farm. In the 1960s, 31 bungalows were built in Woolstrop Way and nine in Davillian Court, off Sims Lane.

Figure 7 – Sims Bridge on the Gloucester & Sharpness Canal

Elmore Lane

This is near to Sims Lane, also in the north, off the west side of Bristol Road. This leads to the River Severn (see page 9) and the village of Elmore. It was also affected by the making of the canal that closed the thoroughfare to Elmore until 1827. Once over the canal this lane runs alongside the banks of the River Severn and is the best place to witness the Severn Bore. This road is now closed at Bristol Road and access is now via the small set of traffic lights north of Elmore Lane.

School Lane

School Lane, formerly Longney Lane, is the location of St James' Church (see page 33), Field Court Estate (see page 59) and was the location of many Quedgeley Schools (see page 82).

Originally, School Lane went to the north of St James' Church and onto the village of Longney. This lane also had lots of problems due to the building of the canal from 1794 to 1827.

A Rectory was built in 1840, next to St James' Church.

The lane was diverted south of the Church in 1841 and from that point onwards, Longney Lane was known as School Lane.

Naas Lane

Naas Lane is further down the Bristol Road on the east side, south of Quedgeley. Naas Lane was likely to have been there before the eighteenth century, always leading to Brookthorpe.

In 1915 the Government purchased land to build the National Filling Factory No. 5 (see page 60) at Manor Farm.

After World War I, as mentioned in the history of Manor Farm (see page 53), a Ploughing and Horticulture Training School was set up at the farm for wounded veterans.

In 1939, the Secretary of State for Air acquired the same land at Manor Farm from Gloucestershire County Council to build the RAF Maintenance Unit (see page 62).

There are many houses and bungalows along the north side of the lane and Needham Avenue was added after 1939 to provide 38 houses for serving police officers.

At the top of Naas Lane in the east, the Dow-Mac Concrete Factory opened in 1963. They operated for many years making precast concrete railway sleepers. They closed around 1990 with the loss of 110 jobs. The large area of land is still used as an industrial site, with the railway line acting as the Quedgeley boundary.

Waterways
The River Severn
The great River Severn comes into being as a little stream, 2,000 feet above sea level near the bare summit of Plynlimon, Wales.

The length of the Severn is 220 miles, making it the longest river in Britain. It is joined by several rivers before it reaches its end at the Bristol Channel. The banks on the River Severn, at Stonebench in Quedgeley, are said to be one of the best places to watch the truly spectacular natural phenomena known as The Severn Bore.

Figure 8 – The Severn Bore at Stonebench

The Severn Bore is a large tidal surge in the River Severn estuary, where the tidal range is the second highest in the world. It is formed when the rising tide moves into the funnel shaped Bristol Channel and Severn Estuary. The surging water then forges up stream in a series of waves, as far as Gloucester. Surfing takes place on the waves and it has been known for a surfer to ride on the wave for seven miles.

Figure 9 – Surfing on The Severn Bore

The spring tide (not related to the season) can reach a height of six feet as the riverbanks get narrower towards Minsterworth and Stonebench in Quedgeley. The water rises 10 feet at full tide. The name Bore appears to have come from the Scandinavian word Bara, meaning a billow, wave or swell. The best Bores are often around Good Friday. This is because Good Friday falls near the vernal equinox, when tides run high. Easter Sunday is always the first Sunday after the full moon, which happens upon or next after, the twenty-first day of March. There are approximately 250 Bores every year, two a day on about 130 days of the year. The Bores come in groups of three and four days at a time, according to the lunar month. The best Bores are always in February-March-April and August-September-October. If you go to watch the Bore, wear suitable clothes and shoes. The Bore often comes over the bank onto Elmore Lane.

In 1607, a Tsunami came into the Bristol Channel and continued up the River Severn, drowning 2,000 people. It took cottages, animals and trees with it. Churches marked their walls to show how high the water reached.

The River Severn has been sailed on by trows and other vessels for hundreds of years. The waters were very difficult to sail in and took a long time to get anywhere. When it was a low tide, the Captain would have to tie up, sometimes for days to wait for the next high tide. There were several inns along the banks from Gloucester to the Bristol Channel. The Stonebench Inn was on the riverbank, on the border of the villages of Elmore and Quedgeley.

The name Stonebench came about because there is a bench of stone, three quarters of the way across the river, from Quedgeley to Minsterworth.

The Gloucester & Sharpness Canal

By the end of the eighteenth century there was a demand for a canal to be built to bypass the River Severn from Gloucester to Berkeley. Trade was good, vessels were getting bigger and travelling overseas. The canal would cut through Quedgeley and run parallel and close to the River Severn. The canal was designed by the Civil Engineer, Robert Mylne, and Parliament granted the sum of £200,000 for the canal to be built. It was started in 1794. Robert Mylne left in 1798. By 1818, the canal had reached Stank Bridge in Hardwicke. It was completed in 1827 at a cost of between £432,000 and £440,000. It is 16 miles long, 16 feet deep, lined with blue clay and originally it had 16 wooden swing bridges. Each bridge had a home built for the bridge operator and his family. Not all the vessels used the canal in the beginning, because they did not like paying the dues and the River Severn was free to sail on. The canal did not reach Berkeley as planned, instead it ended at Sharpness. Can you imagine the inconvenience farmers and parishioners had for 33 years with the canal cutting through their land?

In between World Wars I and II, wooden week-end bungalows were built on the banks of the canal. Locals came to swim in the canal. After 1945, many bungalows were lived in permanently. For many years Tom Priday was the Bridge Man at Rea Bridge in Elmore Lane. He would push the bridge open to let the barges through, loaded with timber, coal and grain. Shell-Mex and John Harker's Company had many barges coming through daily. Local farmers left their milk churns by the bridge, then a boat would collect them and deliver them to Cadbury's Factory at Frampton-on-Severn.

Gradually there were fewer commercial barges on the canal. Pleasure boats then filled the Gloucester docks and the moorings along the banks of the canal.

Figure 10 – Pleasure boats on the Gloucester & Sharpness Canal

For many years Moreland's Match Factory on the Bristol Road in Gloucester rented the part of the canal which was on the borders of Hempsted and Quedgeley. Huge logs floated there, which would later be used in their Gloucester factory to make England's Glory Matches.

These days there are less bridge operators and their surplus homes have been sold to private buyers.

In recent years, Gloucester has organised several Tall Ship Festivals in the Docks which have been very successful. Tall Ships have come hundreds of miles to take part and they stay several days for people to climb aboard them.

The Tall Ships enter the Bristol Channel and when they reach Sharpness Docks they lock into the Gloucester & Sharpness Canal and travel to Gloucester Quays. The residents enjoy seeing them pass slowly through Quedgeley.

Figure 11 – Tall Ship on the Gloucester & Sharpness Canal

Chapter 3 – Our History

The area south of Gloucester was probably a wooded route from the Cotswolds, down to the River Severn. Who arrived in this area first, we ask?

Historians tell us that in the Stone, Bronze and Iron Ages, it was home for thousands of itinerants and immigrants, but we do not have sufficient evidence to write about them. They would have survived on wild animals, fish from the rivers and fruit from the trees and bushes.

600 BC – 500 AD

Over the centuries Britain was constantly invaded by soldiers rowing across the waters in their long boats. Finally, the Celtic tribes arrived in Britain sometime between 600 BC and 500 BC. They stayed for hundreds of years and had their own language, Kings and Queens. This all ended when the Roman Emperor Claudius invaded Britain with thousands of his soldiers in the first century.

Britain was now Rome's most northerly outpost. The soldiers built a fortress at Kingsholm, Gloucester in 49 AD. It was the lowest practical crossing point of the River Severn to Wales. In 65 AD the soldiers moved into the centre of the town and built a second fortress. They laid straight roads, heading out to the north and south. The Roman road going south took the route through the land that today we call Hempsted, Quedgeley and Hardwicke. In Quedgeley, the road passed through today's Carters Orchard, Tesco Superstore, St James' Churchyard, Church Drive and beyond. We can deduce from this that the Romans were probably the first people to arrive in Quedgeley. The Roman road is marked on old Ordnance maps. Part of the Quedgeley Roman road was discovered on the east side of the B4008 recently and a Roman farmstead built in the first century was also found.

The Roman Army later moved their Headquarters over the River Severn to Caerleon near Newport, leaving behind their retired soldiers.

By the second century, the remaining Roman architects planned streets and fine houses in the town. They changed the Gloucester's Celtic name of Caer-Glow, to Glevum.

The remains of a third century Roman Villa and a coffin containing a skeleton, were found at Cobe Medical Equipment factory, on the Olympus Business Park development in Quedgeley in 1995.

In the fifth century, the Roman Emperor Honorius and his army left Britain's shores. They had taken on more than they could rule. Things deteriorated. The land and the British inhabitants suffered.

The Angles and Saxons from Northern Europe and Vikings from Norway came seeking to conquer the country. They made the best of the old buildings the Romans had left behind. Soon they had a permanent presence in Britain. They made great changes to the country and were well received. The country was now called Angloland.

A Saxon Chief called Cwoed was said to live south of Glevum. It was a place where Glevum's refuse was burnt. More recently, the Gloucestershire County Archivist's translation was *"a clearing, or fields belonging to the Saxon Chief called Cwoed"*. This is the area now known as Quedgeley. The River Severn was called Sabrina.

501 AD – 1800 AD

There was a chapel in Quedgeley before 1095 when the parish was formed. In the twelfth century land was given to the chapel upon which St James' Church (see page 33) was built in 1210. In 1327 King Edward II was murdered at Berkeley Castle. I wonder how many of the 12 people living in Quedgeley at that time, came out to line the highway and pay their respects to the King, as his body was taken to St Peter's Abbey in Gloucester to be laid to rest. Later the highway was called Kings Way. In 1348 approximately 30% of the population had died of starvation and Black Death in England. In 1535 King Henry VIII and Queen Anne Boleyn visited the parish and were met by representatives of the City of Gloucester. In 1551 the population of Quedgeley had grown to 69, and in 1603 it was 123.

1801 AD – 1850 AD

By 1801 the population of Quedgeley had risen to 203.

In the beginning of the nineteenth century, Quedgeley Parish had 20 people who received poor–relief regularly and 10 occasionally, the cost was £215. By 1832 the annual cost had risen to £229. Quedgeley became part of the Gloucester Poor Law Union in 1835.

There were many small traders in the parish: boot and shoemakers, butchers, bakers, beer retailers, a black smith, cider retailer, corn and flour dealer, cattle dealer, hay dealer, grocers, a tax collector, a wheel wright and at least eight farmers at any one time.

The Bristol and Gloucester Railway was built through Quedgeley in 1844. In Naas Lane, a large brick bridge was built to enable parishioners to pass under the railway line. Many years later, a level crossing was laid nearby together with opening gates and a large wooden signal box. The lane was diverted and the bridge was not used. A signalman and his family lived close to the crossing. Time passed and the crossing and gates were removed and the traffic went back under the bridge.

1851 AD – 1950 AD

The Boat Inn, now called Friar Tucks, was the only licenced property in Quedgeley by 1889. In 1908 Mr Guilding was landlord of The Boat Inn. Albert Job Such in 1911 and by 1921, John Ivor Edwards became the landlord for many years. . It was renamed The Plough Hotel and remained the only inn until 1985 when the Basket Maker was built on the Bristol Road at the new Tesco roundabout (see page 78).

Figure 12 – The Plough Hotel circa 1900

Figure 13 – Customer outing from the Plough Hotel circa 1925

Figure 14 – Tea-time at the Plough Hotel circa 1932

Figure 15 – Another outing from the Plough Hotel circa 1950

As the twentieth century progressed and cars replaced horses and traps, more visitors passed through the centre of Gloucester. Whether they were travelling north, south, east or west, many had to pass through Quedgeley. In 1914 the first bus route served Quedgeley. William Gardner (the owner of the bus) ran the service from Frampton to Gloucester. His young daughter Ivy was a part-time bus conductress. Gilbert Nash was one of the first drivers. Quedgeley soon had a petrol filling station in the north and the south of the parish. A bus service was set up in the 1920s between Gloucester and Bristol, which was welcomed. Later a private bus company from Saul called Silvey's ran a regular service to Gloucester every day. You could also have a canal pleasure trip between Gloucester and Sharpness on the paddle steamers named Wave or Lapwing.

In 1921 Mrs J Roach was running the newly-built Retreat Guest House on Bristol Road. Many more bed and breakfast places then opened along the busy Bristol Road. The Retreat Guest House was the first bed and breakfast accommodation built for travellers breaking their journey (mainly between the north and the south) and it was very busy until the war broke out in 1939 and petrol was rationed. It was where my husband and I lived and ran a B&B business between 1959 and 1982.

Figure 16 – The Retreat Guest House

From the 1920s onwards Quedgeley always managed to put a football team together. By 1930 Quedgeley had a population of 912 people.

Figure 17 – Quedgeley Rovers AFC Team, 1925-26 season

In November 1932 land was transferred to the people of Quedgeley by the Curtis-Hayward family for a recreation ground in the centre of the parish. It had a set of three swings and a wooden plank bench. Mr and Mrs Arch lived in the cottage next to the field and he locked the swings up on a Sunday.

In the 1930s cricket was played at Field Court Farm, School Lane. In Figure 18 we can identify Mr Phelps and Mr Wixey (in the front row, fourth and fifth from the left) and Mrs Phelps seated in front of the team.

Figure 18 – Quedgeley Cricketers, 1934

Mains water, electricity and gas had been installed by 1935. New development started to emerge along the Bristol Road.

A popular eating place called Brook's Transport café opened next to the Plough Hotel during the Second World War. It was a place where large vehicles could pull in for a good meal and often parked overnight. After the war the café catered for coaches that travelled from Birmingham to Weston-Super-Mare for the day and then catered for them on their return journey. The café was seriously damaged by a fire; the site was cleared and a new café was built in the adjoining lorry park. The Plough Hotel also did a lot of catering.

In the 1940s Marion Macloud ran a Dancing School in Quedgeley Village Hall and put on shows. Many residents enjoyed the shows during the year. As a child I used to attend the dancing classes. In Figure 19 I am Snow White on the left.

Figure 19 – A show from Marion Macloud's Dancing School

In January, February and March 1947, Gloucestershire had heavy rainfalls that caused the worst flooding for years. This was followed by snow and more rain. The River Severn overflowed and was 15 feet above normal level. Residents in Quedgeley living by the river were evacuated.

1951 AD – 2000 AD

In 1950, due to the inclement weather, the Church fête was held in the Village Hall. In Figure 20, I do a bit of fishing with Gordon Parmenter, Terry Hogarth, Richard Cale, the Rector's son and Dorothy Barrow. Behind Dorothy we can see Margaret Tracey (née Cale) and Ann Cobb. I am pictured on the far left.

Figure 20 – Church fête in the First Quedgeley Village Hall, 1950

On 6 February 1952 King George VI died and Princess Elizabeth became Queen. The Coronation took place on 2 June 1953 and we celebrated in Quedgeley. A television set was positioned in the original Quedgeley Village Hall. Only a handful of homes in Quedgeley had a TV in 1953. Local pensioners were taken to the Hall at 9:45am to watch the London proceedings. Later they enjoyed a sit-down lunch of ham, tongue, salad, trifles, fruit, jellies and cream, followed by cheese and biscuits, soft drinks or beer. At 2:40pm there was a highland dancing demonstration and at 8:00pm a social with games and dancing. All these entertainments were free.

Children assembled in the Church of England School in School Lane (now the Youth and Community Centre) in fancy dress and, led by a pipe band, headed down to the Bristol Road Recreation Ground where there was a service conducted by the Rector, the Revd F J Lanham. In Figure 21 (on page 21) we see the line-up waiting to find out who had won the fancy dress competition. We see (left to right): Mr C Taylor, myself, Mr and Mrs Wanklin and daughter Ester in front of them. Figure 22 shows Elaine Brint and Jennifer Ely, two of the competitors. After the fancy dress was judged, sports were held in the grounds. The children had ham and eggs, cakes, ice-cream and soft drinks for tea. Later, souvenir beakers were handed out.

Teenagers had their sports at 4:15pm but, unlike the youngsters and pensioners, they had to pay for refreshments from a stall. In the evening the teenagers were invited to the Village Hall with everyone else. Adults were expected to do their share of sports, but this did not take place until 6:00pm. A slow cycle race was part of the excitement.

Chapter 3 – Our History   Page 21

Figure 21 – Coronation Celebration fancy dress   *Figure 22 – Elaine Brint and Jennifer Ely in fancy dress*

Many went to the social in the Hall to finish off the day. The main attractions were the Gloucester Pipe Band, the Patterson Highland Dancers and Mrs Hunt's band which played at the social. To organise all the events, a Coronation Committee was formed. It consisted of a Sports Committee, a Pensioners' Committee, a Social Committee and a Decorations Committee. Some of the Committee members were Mr Stroud, Miss Pready, Mrs Calf, Mrs Hooper, Mrs Boulter, Mrs Nelmes and Mrs Ely, and some of their families are still in Quedgeley today. A good time was had by the young and the not-so-young, but I seem to remember it finished up with rain.

Harry Gage, the local showman, lived in Quedgeley and put on a film show once a week in the Village Hall. In Figure 23 we can see Harry (in the front row with his hands on his lap) with his family. Behind them (left to right) are Ken Meek and myself, Sybil and Herbert Ely, Linda Lawrence and Tom Fox (Harry's grandson).

Figure 23 – Harry Gage in the First Quedgeley Village Hall

In 1952/53, the Rural District Council started building council houses in School Lane named 1-16 Parklands, followed in 1955 with 26 flats at the rear of the houses. A red telephone kiosk was located on the pavement in front of the houses. This was a great help as not many people had phones then.

One night in 1958, Quedgeley's first Village Hall completely burnt down. It took four years of fundraising before the Hall was replaced. Village events were held in the Red Cross Centre, The Scouts' Hut, The Rectory and the Methodist Chapel.

In 1961 the Gloucester Rural District Council had bought land from St James' Church and built 10 retirement bungalows at St James Close in School Lane. Later 12 more bungalows were added. Graham Johnson, a past St James Close warden, provided me with the brief history shown in Figure 24 and Figure 25 (on page 23).

St James Close

In 1961, the Housing and Planning Committee of Gloucester Rural District Council, in their search for land on which to build bungalows for retired people, approached the incumbent of Quedgeley, who agreed to the sale of .68 acres sufficient for ten bungalows.

The land was a portion of the Rectory House Grounds which lay between the Rectory Drive on the West, the main Bristol Road on the East and School Lane on the South.

Whilst a boundary hedge to the North separated the land of Woolstrop Farm.

Ten Retired Persons Bungalows were designed by Demuth L.R.J.B.A. Built by the firm of Ashmores at a cost of £17,500 and laid out in the form of a crescent fronting School Lane, to suit the shape of the site. The old trees of Oak and Chestnut bordering School Lane were retained and the area within the crescent laid out as lawn. By April 1962, the first occupants were in residence and cultivated their little gardens in front of their windows.

Meanwhile, the Rural District Council had negotiated the purchase of the remaining 1.84 acres of the above land which contained the Old Stable Buildings, Kitchen Garden, Orchard and Paddock of the Rectory.

Planning permission could not be obtained for more than ten further bungalows with a Wardens House and Community Centre Building, so the Old stables and Kitchen Garden were happily adapted to form an Estate Management Depot much needed by the Council.

Figure 24 – St James Close Notes (page 1)

Chapter 3 – Our History   Page 23

In Figure 25 I believe the reference to Mrs U J Newman as Warden near the end of the page should read Mrs U J Norman.

> *The layout of the new site was also on the open plan, the Wardens House and Community Centre forming the central building with the bungalows arranged attractively in pairs around the area. The layout also overcame the difficulty that the Highways Authority would not allow any new road to be built into the area from School Lane.*
>
> *This problem was resolved by redesigning the Rectory Drive to form a new approach road curving into the centre of the new area and ending in a cul-de-sac in front of the Wardens House. This proved to be equally convenient for the Rectory, Bungalows and the Estate Maintenance Depot.*
>
> *The style of design of this second group of buildings were different from the first and building costs had also risen considerably.*
>
> *The architect responsible for them was J.F.Owen-Pawson and the building contractors were Messrs Uzzell & Morgan Ltd. The total cost amounted to £30,093 and the houses were occupied by October 1964.*
>
> *Mrs. U. J. Newman Was appointed to the post of Warden.*
>
> *As the bungalows lie happily in the shadow of the 13th Century Spire of the Parish Church of St James, Quedgeley, the name of St James Close was chosen for the community.*
>
> \#
>
> *This is a copy of the original framed text that was hanging up in the Community Room of St James Close*   G F J

Figure 25 – St James Close Notes (page 2)

In 1962 the Birmingham to Bristol stretch of the M5 was completed. This took a lot of traffic off the local roads.

In 1963 the Shell-Mex & BP Organisation built a large fuel distribution centre on the borders of Quedgeley and Hardwicke in School Lane. It was a 30-acre site at the side of the Gloucester & Sharpness Canal. A large two-storey office block was situated at the entrance.

Large tankers carrying up to 123,000 tons of fuel came and unloaded into 28 vertical storage tanks. The centre replaced The Regent Oil Company's smaller site at Monk Meadow in Hempsted, Gloucester. The new distribution site increased the workload of many local bridge operators. The canal banks suffered with the continued wash and had to be shored up with interlocking steel girders.

The large lorries would arrive at the centre, collect their fuel and then deliver it to garages in the region. School Lane was the only road available at the time and suffered with the increase in traffic going backwards and forwards. The local school children had to be very careful.

The distribution centre was a fire risk and a high earth bank was built beside School Lane to protect the nearby houses in Hardwicke. Eventually the centre was demolished and houses were built on the site. The lorries then had to go to Avonmouth to collect their fuel.

Figure 26 – B.P. Miller, one of the many Petrol Tankers

January 1963 was the coldest winter since 1814. On 11 January 1963 it was -11.1° Celsius, on 22 January 1963 it was down to -17.2° Celsius. The Gloucester & Sharpness Canal froze. Tugs Mayflower and Primrose used icebreakers. Temperatures went down to -20.1° Celsius. From memory, we had snow and ice for 50 days and it made it the worst winter of the century. The snow fell on Boxing Day and it was still on the ground six weeks later.

At the time, my husband and I lived at The Retreat Guest House on the Bristol Road, and we had a house full of Dutch engineers who were working for a firm called Land & Marine. The engineers were tunnelling under the Gloucester & Sharpness Canal, at the two-mile bend, in Quedgeley. They had to continually break the ice before they could dive in and lay pipes. When they returned at the end of the day, it was hot baths and cooked dinners.

The bedrooms were all fitted out with electric fires and coin meters. We did not have central heating 50 years ago. With 10 bedrooms all with fires on, we were lucky not to freeze up.

In Gloucester, Rugby and football matches were held up to 22 December 1962 and then cancelled for weeks. Forage harvesters were brought in to clear the snow on the Gloucester City Ground. Greyhound racing stopped on the Boxing Day meeting, but later the use of straw chaff and tarpaulins enabled the dogs to run again on 19 January 1963.

The demand for bricks dried up as building operations were suspended. At Broadmoor Brickworks near Cinderford, the kilns were put out of action when a million bricks had piled up. The unbroken freeze cut off the water supply to countless homes and havoc was created when the pipes thawed out. It also froze the rivers, canals and made the roads into skating rinks. There was a 20 feet drift at Windy Corner, near Kingscote, and the biggest icicle was the one produced by a burst main at Coberley, near Crickley Hill. Roads were blocked all over the county and snow ploughs were out night and day helping cut off villagers who were getting short of food.

The first Severn Bridge was opened in 1966. This meant traffic travelling between the south of England and Wales no longer had to come through Quedgeley and Gloucester to get over the River Severn. This made a huge difference to the amount of traffic travelling on the Bristol Road.

In 1967 Quedgeley was still not connected to the main sewage system but eventually this changed. In Figure 27 we see some of the residents discussing the route it was going to take: (left to right) Mr T Sellick, Mr Marsh, Mr F Martin, Mr K Meek talking with Mr E Shropshall of the Gloucester Rural District Council Engineers' Department.

Figure 27 – Residents and surveyor discussing the sewerage system

By 1969 streetlights were installed. Planning started on the Quedgeley bypass from Cole Avenue to M5 junction 12. It was many years before it was built. This was much needed to ease the traffic on the Bristol Road in Quedgeley.

In 1973 Gloucestershire was divided into six District Councils. Quedgeley was moved into the new Stroud District. Parishioners were not pleased. It took a long time to sort the administration and public transport out. The planning and building of many new homes in Quedgeley began at this time.

In 1974 Field Court Farm was developed, followed later by Woolstrop Farm. Quedgeley House was knocked down ready to start building the roads named St James' and Severnvale Drive.

In 1976 Stroud District Council wrote to the residents on Bristol Road informing them that it was no longer sufficient to refer to their houses by house name as this made it difficult for the essential services (doctors, post office, police, ambulance etc.) to locate properties. From 15 November 1976, the houses would be allocated a house number as below. There were gaps to allow for properties being built at the time.

Number	Name	Number	Name
2	Ridge Bourne	29	Fox Mount
4	Southcroft	69	Wainsbridge
6	Rose Mount	71	Old Tiles
8	Edelweiss	73	Pennleigh
10	Holmleigh	75	The Villa Cottage
12	Sad Patch	77	Greenways
14	Belmont	79	Rhodean
16	Kayakers	97	Autocraft
18	Westfield	111	Quedgeley Farm

Chapter 3 – Our History

20	Corner House	121	Quedgeley Garage
34	Green Farm	123	Brooks Café
84	Ingleside	133	The Laurels
86	Gem Croft	137	The Plough Hotel
88	Padova House	139	Reeds Farm
90	May View	141	The Little Thatch
92	Sunnyside	143	Coppins
94	Quinton House	145	Chilterns
96	Tintern House	151	Reads Cottage No. 4
98	The Redlands	153	Reads Cottage No. 5
100	Wynbridge	155	Reads Cottage No. 6
102	Lesscote	157	Reads Cottage No. 7
104	Elder Tree Cottage	159	The Forge
106	Yew Tree Cottage	161	Forge Cottage No. 1
108	The Chantry	163	Forge Cottage No. 2
110	Hilldene	169	Caravan Site
112	Deveron	171	Shop
114	Blenheim	173	Highcliffe Cottage
116	The Retreat	179	Highcliffe Farm
126	Rose Villa No. 2	205	The Bungalow
128	Rose Villa No. 1	211	Chillon
130	Vine House	213	Winton
132	Magnolia Cottage	215	Packers Cottage
134	Yew Tree Villas No. 1	245	The Quarr No. 6
136	Yew Tree Villas No. 2	247	The Quarr No. 4
208	Village Hall	249	The Quarr No. 3
280	The Hawthorns	251	The Quarr No. 1 & 2
290	The Nook	257	Manor Farm No. 1
328	Lawn Cottage No. 1	259	Manor Farm No. 2
330	Lawn Cottage No. 2	273	The Croft
346	The Lawn	277	The White House
354	Birch House Farm	279	Rosedale
372	Glenley	281	Laura Croft
374	Clovelly	285	Berrows Close No. 1
376	Hill View	287	Berrows Close No. 2
378	The Halt	291	Lawnmeir & Caravans
378	Royston Cottage	295	Green Acre
386	Moorhurst Garage	305	Kenloc
388	Orchard Villas No. 1	311	Kevrill House
390	Orchard Villas No. 2	313	The Willows
396	Corruna House No. 1	355	Oriel House

| 398 | Corruna House No. 2 | 357 | Waterwells Villa |

On 14 April 1978 the £2,250,000 link road from Cole Avenue, Gloucester to the M5 Junction 12 at Hardwicke was opened, see Figure 28.

Figure 28 – The opening of the M5 link road

In the early 1980s a party was held at The Old Rectory for Ursula Norman for her sixty-fifth birthday and also her impending retirement after 21 years as Warden of St James' Close in School Lane. In Figure 29 we see (left to right): Murial Hancock (Ursula's mother), Bert and Ursula Norman and Caroline Meek.

Figure 29 – Birthday and Retirement of Ursula Norman

Following the major developments, there was a cry for shops and facilities. Tesco Superstore was opened in 1984 (see page 77) and the adjoining Post Office was also welcomed. The next project was to build new schools (see page 82), to cater for all the children. Severn Vale Comprehensive had to be enlarged. Fieldcourt Church of England Infant School and Fieldcourt Junior School were built in Courtfield Road, followed by Beech Green County Primary School in the road named St James'.

On 9 May 1985 the Basket Maker Pub (see page 78) was opened on the Bristol Road near Tesco.

In 1986 a team of unemployed people started cooking meals in the redundant church school buildings and provided an average of 50 meals per day for the elderly at £1 per meal, see Figure 30. The scheme was sponsored by Stroud District Council and funded with a grant of £50,000 from Manpower Services Commission.

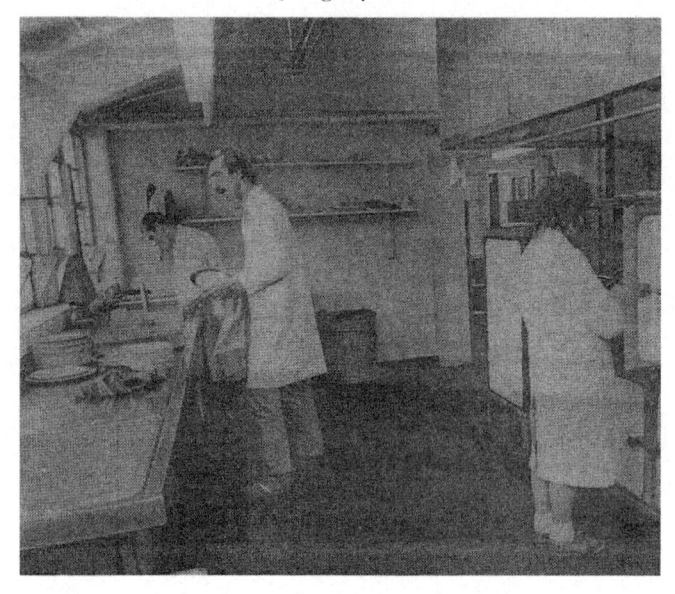

Figure 30 – Manpower Services Commission lunch preparations for the elderly

In the same building in 1987, Manpower Services Commission gave the unemployed who were sent from the Job Centre, a year of training for interior painting, decorating and gardening. Work was carried out for the elderly and disabled in the local villages.

In May 1987 planning permission was granted for a licenced restaurant and lounge bar (now Miller & Carter) at Olympus Park Business Centre at the Tesco roundabout. Stroud District Council also approved an application for a prestige office development on Olympus Park, adjacent to the Cole Avenue roundabout.

In January 1989 D L Tomlins & Sons Ltd opened a meat factory at 123 Bristol Road, Quedgeley. It opened its doors on a Saturday morning to locals to buy fresh meat, and they were always very busy. They had 60 staff and 15 insulated heavy goods vehicles. In the same area there was a large furniture shop. This has all been replaced by Woods Veterinary Group and Farm Foods.

The first turf for the Health Centre on St James' road was cut on 27 January 1989 by Bill Oakes (Chairman of the Family Practitioner Committee) and Rennie Fitchie (Chairman of the Gloucester Health Authority). On 10 August 1989 the new L-shaped Library (see page 79) was opened in the Tesco Car Park. The Village Hall could not cater for all the village bookings and a new Youth and Community Centre (see page 75) was opened in 1995.

Royal Visitors to Gloucester and Quedgeley
Princess Mary Tudor (King Henry VIII's daughter)
Mary Tudor was received by the Mayor and Burgesses (citizens) of the town of

Gloucester on 12 September in the seventeenth year of the reign of our Sovereign Lord King Henry VIII in the time of Mr John Rawlings, Mayor of the same town, Mr William Mathew and Mr Henry French, the Sheriffs there.

First the Mayor, Aldermen and Sheriffs in scarlet and 100 burgesses rode to Quedgeley's Green within the liberty of the said town there keeping array (in order) till the said Princess came and then (made) their obeisance (bow) on horseback, showing one of the maces (staff carried as a mark of authority) of the town. Then, by the advice of their council, Mr Mayor and all his brethren in scarlet setting forward on horseback two and two, the sergeants leading the way foremost and knights, squires and gentlemen in the midst and the Mayor next before Her Grace riding with the sergeant-at-arms bareheaded and one of the sergeant's maces in his hand.

Then all the ladies and gentlewomen following Her Grace on horseback-after them all her servants in a livery (uniform for servants) and her officers, and after them other of the sergeants and burgesses of the town two and two so riding to the town end where all the Clergy were in copes, (priests robes) cross, carpets and cushions and Her Grace lovingly there kissing the cross on horseback.

And they rode forth every man after the said manner through the town bringing Her Grace into the Abbey through Saint Edward's gate, the Abbot and his brethren then being in the Abbey porch with copes, cross, carpets and cushions receiving Her Grace. And so, she did alight off horse and kissed the cross and then went up to the High Altar, Mr Mayor and all his brethren in scarlet going before Her Grace, and there she offered a piece of gold and then parted to her lodging, Mr Mayor and his said brethren before her. Gifts and presents given by the Mayor and his brethren to the princess. First two fat oxen of the best that might be gotten and 10 fat wethers, (male sheep) of the best that might be gotten.

King Henry VIII and Queen Anne Boleyn

They came to Quedgeley in 1534 after spending a week in Gloucester. The King and Queen stayed at the former Abbot's Lodging House, Church House, in Parliament Street, Gloucester. They were met by the Burghers of Gloucester on Quedgeley Green, north of the Church. A Bible was given to the Church at this meeting, but it does not exist now.

Queen Elizabeth I

On 8 August 1574 held Court in Gloucester and slept the night at St Nicholas House in Westgate Street. In 1576 the Queen made a grant of land to Quedgeley Church. The rent was to be used to find a light burning on the altar, and before the image of St James. Queen Elizabeth was in Gloucester again in 1580 and granted the City the Status of a Port, allowing direct trade with foreign ports via the River Severn.

Queen Mary

Queen Mary, the widow of King George V, paid a visit to No. 7 Maintenance Unit, RAF Quedgeley. The Queen was taken around the Unit by Group Captain E R Wood, Station Commander from June 1941 to July 1942.

Queen Elizabeth II

The late Queen made a private visit to watch the Severn Bore at Stonebench, Elmore Lane, Quedgeley, in the 1950s. It was very informal, and not many people were there.

Dukes of Gloucester

Henry and his son Richard, both came to No. 7 Maintenance Unit Headquarters, RAF Quedgeley on separate occasions (Henry in 1958, Richard in 1978).

Princess Margaret Rose (Queen Elizabeth II's sister)

Arrived at Quedgeley's Scouts and Cubs Headquarters in School Lane in 1988, see Figure 94 (on page 97). The Lord-Lieutenant of Gloucestershire also attended. The Princess had a big welcome and duly officially opened the Headquarters.

H.R.H. Prince of Wales

On 4 June 2003 Prince Charles (now King Charles III) opened the Tri-Service Centre at Waterwells Site, Quedgeley. The Fire, Ambulance and Police Services shared the facilities. The cost was £6,300,000. In 2005 the Fire Services moved to Taunton.

Chapter 4 – Our Buildings

St James' Church

The Church is the oldest surviving building in Quedgeley. Although it was not mentioned in the Domesday Book 1085, Quedgeley was most likely included in the Gloucester Abbey's Standish or Haresfield Estates. They were held by Durand, Sheriff of Gloucester in 1086. Quedgeley had a Chapel in 1087 and there was some parochial independence established by 1095.

In 1137, Earl Milo, Constable of Gloucester, gave all the tithes of Quedgeley Church to the Canons of Llanthony, Gloucester. This settlement continued until the reign of King Henry VIII.

The first Minister at St James' Church was called Walter, in 1210. The Church was dedicated to St James and St Mary Magdalene. It was a small building in the beginning, of ashlar, with a Cotswold stone roof. The Church was also given land in this century.

By 1370 we read that the Chaplain of Quedgeley was a Graduate. Ministers over the years have been named Chaplain, Vicar and Rector.

In 1538 King Henry VIII's reformation ordered church records to be kept. By 1541 the King had dissolved St Peter's Abbey which then became Gloucester Cathedral. The new Diocese of Gloucester was formed and Quedgeley was part of the Diocese. In 1551 there were 69 communicants attending the Parish Church. From 1559, all Roman Catholics were turned away.

In 1563 there were 28 households in Quedgeley. The Church registers date from 1559 and are complete, apart from 1751 to 1812. By 1603 there were now 123 communicants at St James' Church. In 1650 Quedgeley had grown to 40 families.

Revd John Makepeace held the living in 1662 but was said to have been out of his senses for many years before he died. He is buried below the altar. In 1683 an Act was passed that Quedgeley Rectory now belonged to The Right Honourable Talbot, Earl of Sussex. In 1750 the Curate P Bons held a living in Lincolnshire as well as Quedgeley. Services were held alternately in the mornings and afternoons. He is also buried below the altar in 1770.

There has been a great variety of Patrons of the Living, which until quite recently was a 'Donative'; this gave the Patron the right to nominate to the Living, without the Bishop having to institute the Incumbent. Amongst many names of the Patrons are found The Dukes of Manchester and The Earl of Warwick. In the eighteenth century the parish really started to grow. By 1801 it had 203 parishioners; in 1831 this had jumped to 297 and was up to 401 parishioners in 1851.

Inside the building

The South Aisle
Later called the Lady Chapel, this was built in the fourteenth century. It has been held by the Barrow and the Hayward families. Both families have large wall monuments erected in their honour. Deal pews were added in 1857.

The Church Tower
The Church Tower was built after the South Aisle in the late fourteenth century, with a solid octagonal broach spire which housed a peal of six bells, cast in 1732. Two more bells were added in 1891. All were rehung in 1956. The seventh bell was recast in 1977. The Dedication Service took place on 9 October 1977 by Robert, Bishop of Tewkesbury. All bells were removed, retuned and rehung on a new metal frame in 1994. There is a clock on the south outside wall of the Tower. Below the Tower, inside the Church, is an ancient South Arcade which leads into the South Aisle.

The Chancel
The Chancel is said to have been Jacobean. 1500 to 1650, with an inserted fifteenth century window. It has a panelled ceiling. The eastern panels having carved bosses. The Chancel was rebuilt in 1856 by Henry Woodyer. A heavy wooden door now leads to the new kitchen on the north wall. There is a stone Reredos, a sculpture representation of the Last Supper, at the altar, a gift of the Revd T Peters of Earlington for the re-opening of the Church in 1857.

Figure 31 – St James' Church Reredos

Mrs Curtis-Hayward from Quedgeley House presented a rich altar cloth in 1857. The altar and sanctuary areas are paved with Minton encaustic tiles.

The Nave

The nave was added to the Church at a later date. It is sympathetic to the much older Medieval Tower and South Aisle. It has cradle roof timbers, which were possibly re-used. The carved oak fittings were restored in 1856.

Figure 32 – St James' Church Nave and Pews

We hear many stories, even these days, of people sitting in their 'own pews' but in 1512 two families in Quedgeley took it to the extreme. Arthur Porter was at The Manor in 1512, east of the Kings Way. In 1532 there was a dispute between Arthur and Richard Barrow over the right of Richard, who lived in Field Court Hardwicke, to attend St James' Church. The Barrow family had been attending the Church each Sunday but Arthur believed Richard should attend Hardwicke Church instead. Arthur had Richard removed from his pew. The case was tried in the Court of the Star Chamber in London.

The Pulpit and the Choir Stalls

The Pulpit was installed in the seventeenth century. It incorporates carved Jacobean woodwork. The Choir Stalls were later removed.

Figure 33 – St James' Church Pulpit and Choir Stalls

The North Aisle

The North Aisle and North Door were added in 1857 to the existing Nave to house the increased population of the Church. The pews are of a simple structure.

The Porches

Originally, Longney Lane passed on the north side of the Church. The entrance to the Church was via the North Door. In 1780 there was a timber north porch.

Figure 34 – St James' Church North Porch

In 1841 Longney Lane was diverted to the south side of the Church. The South Door was then used as the Church entrance and a timber porch was added in 1857.

Figure 35 – St James' Church South Porch

The Font
The Font was given by the Revd Winstone Hayward for the reopening of the Church in 1857. It is a cylindrical font, encased in an octagonal ashlar casing, with panels of gold and coloured tesserae, including blue forest stone. It has a Jacobean cover.

The Vestry
Built between 1887 and 1891. An inscription on the wall reads, *"The Nave and Chancel of this Church were built and the North Aisle added, in the year of Our Lord 1857"* W F F Knollys Rector, J Curtis-Hayward & James Browning, Churchwardens.

Organ Chamber and Organ
These were added in 1888. The Organ Chamber was built to designs by E Gambier Parry. The Organ, built by Mr Willis of London, comprised four stops in the great, three swell, pedal bourdon, three couplers and two composition pedals. It was a two-manual instrument. The entrance to the chamber was by two 'shoulder arches' supported by one shaft. In May 1995 it was decided that the Willis Organ would be superseded by a modern electronic organ, to be placed at the back of the Nave, together with the speakers. The Organ Chamber became a meeting room, and a kitchen and separate toilet were created.

Memorials
An early memorial to Mr Richard Berow (later Barrow) dated 1562 is over the main South Door, inside the church. In the South Aisle is an elaborate mural monument, dated 1696, to William Hayward. In the Nave, on the south wall near the Organ, is an ornate memorial to Thomas and Elinor Hayward of Woolstrop Manor.

Brasses
In 1532 Arthur Porter placed a medieval brass plaque on the south wall in the Chancel in memory of his two daughters. There are Bazett family brasses on the southwest wall in the Nave. In the North Aisle, on the north wall is a small brass plaque in memory of Canon Herbert and Edith Hadow.

Stained-glass windows
The Lady Chapel
On the east wall, a fine window depicts St Luke and the Virgin Mary in medieval glass, in restored tracery. Inscription Benjamin & Mary Harrison 1856.

The Chancel
In the Chancel the east window, above the main altar, was painted by Messrs Hardman in memory of the Revd W Adams, representing the Crucifixion and Resurrection, see Figure 36 (on page 39). The inscription says *"INRI Iesus Nazarenus Rex Iudaeorum"* meaning Jesus of Nazareth, King of the Jews. There are three smaller windows on the south wall in the chancel.

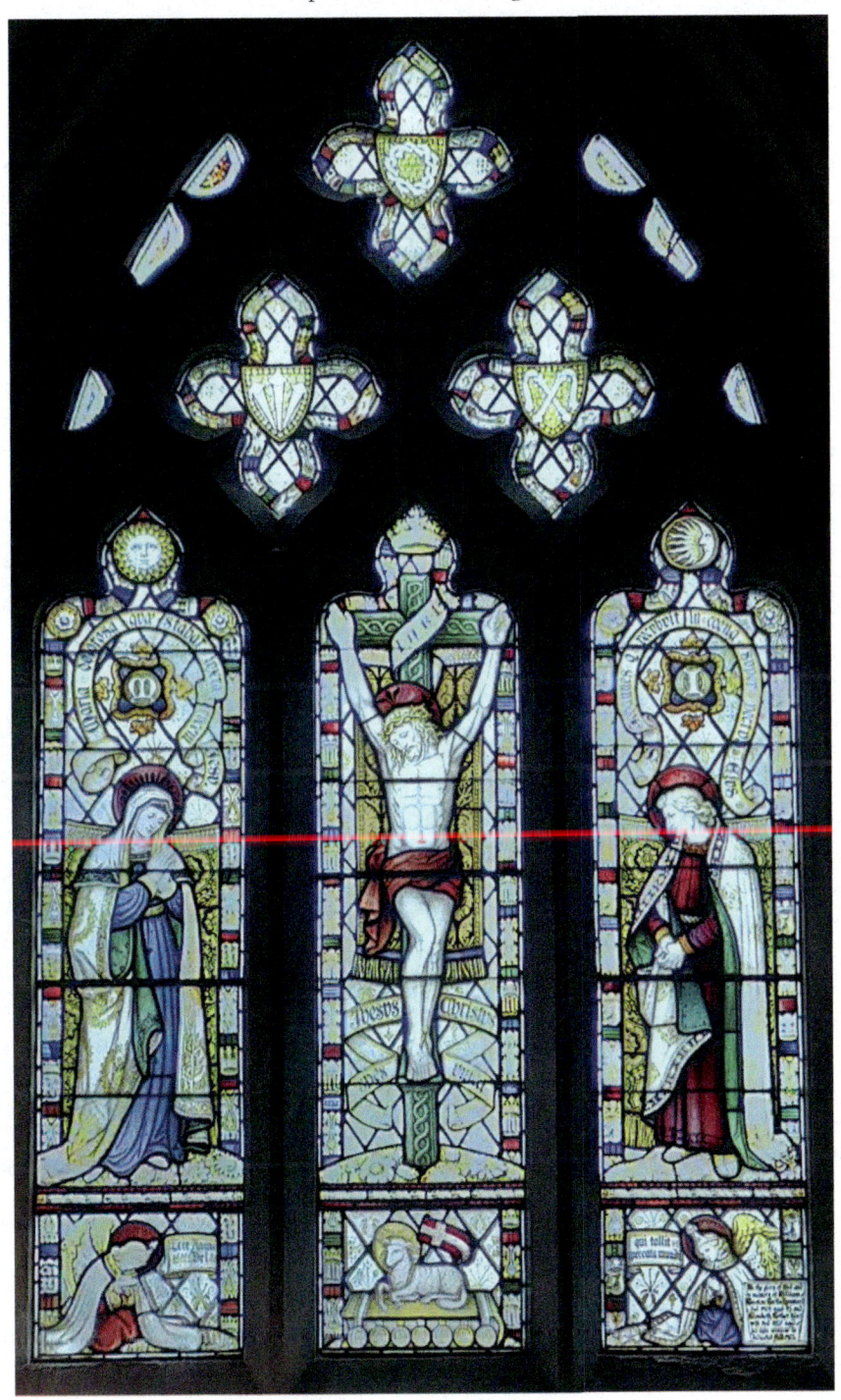

Figure 36 – St James' Church Chancel, East Window

The Vestry
In the vestry the glass window depicts Good Friday and Easter Day.

North Aisle
On the north wall front part of the Aisle, the stained-glass window is of the Nativity with Mary and Jesus. North wall, rear of the North Aisle, the glass depicts the Annunciation with the Virgin Mary and Gabriel. The west window in the North Aisle is by Henry Woodyer; St George is on the left, St Christopher in the centre and St Alban on the right.

The Nave
Rear window is by Charles Eamer Kempe, 1837 to 1907.

Outside the building
Churchyard
The Churchyard contains several large stone memorial graves.

Unfortunately, the inscriptions have faded over the centuries. The Churchyard is closed for any new graves.

The west side has many rows of recent graves with headstones. The east side has a few headstones but is full. Many years ago a Bier Cart was kept in the north corner of the Churchyard.

Figure 37 was the view from Dawes Farm, now Church Drive, and Figure 38 (on page 41) shows a modern drone view of the Church.

Figure 37 – St James' Churchyard (ancient view)

Figure 38 – St James' Churchyard (modern view)

The Quedgeley War Memorial
This stands in the Churchyard, by the gate in School Lane.

Figure 39 – St James' Church War Memorial

The Roll of Honour for World War I (1914-1918)
Arthur Beacall. Second Lieutenant 10th Bn. Attd. 11th Bn. East Lancashire Regiment. Died Saturday, 1 July 1916, aged 20. Buried at the Euston Rd Cemetery, Colincamps, Somme, France. Grave or Reference Panel Number 1.D.6. Son of Thomas & Eleanor Rebecca Beacall of 44 Podsmead Road, Gloucester.

Alan Beacall. Private 2000060 28th Bn. Canadian Infantry (Saskatchewan Regt.) Died Friday, 6 September 1918, aged 25. Buried Aubigny Communal Cemetery Extension, Pas de Calais, France. Grave 1 Number. IV. A. 43. Son of Thomas & Eleanor Beacall, of Quedgeley, Gloucester.

Guy Brooks. 2nd Lieutenant Royal Flying Corps. (Transferred from 3rd Btn. Duke of Wellington's West Riding Regm.) Died 26 March 1918. Buried in Huddersfield

Lockwood Cemetery, Yorkshire, England. (36 World War I casualties were buried in this civic cemetery).

Kenneth Dalziel Brown. Private 240063 1/5th. Gloucesters. Private 47224 1st Btn Royal Enniskillen Fusiliers. Killed in action on 27 July 1918. Buried in Mont Noir Military Cemetery, St Jans-Cappel Nord, France. Grave Number 1.E.12. He was killed in action whilst serving with the Royal Enniskillen Fusiliers.

Bernard Browning. Lance Corporal 2873 4th Bn. Australian Infantry, A.I.F. Died 16 August 1916. Buried in Quedgeley Church Yard, Gloucester, England. To North West of Church.

Charles. E. Cale. Private 18642 12th Battalion Gloucestershire Regiment. Died 4 October 1917. Buried at the Tyne Cot Cemetery. Panel Number 72-75.

Cary Carter. Private 2004 Royal Gloucestershire Hussars. Died at Salt Lake on 21 August 1915, aged 20. Buried in Green Hill Cemetery, Turkey. Grave Number II.C.19. the son of Louis. E. & A. M. Carter of Woolstrop Farm Quedgeley, Gloucester.

Reginald Davis. Private 17460 10th BN. Gloucestershire Regiment. Died Monday, 25 September 1916, aged 23. Buried Etaples Military Cemetery, Pas De Calais, France. Grave Number X1. B. 6. Eldest son of George & Emma Davis, of Brooklyn VILLA, Naas Lane Crossing, Quedgeley, Gloucester. Native of Hardwicke, Gloucester.

George Farmer. Private P/O1553(S) 2nd. R.M.Bn. R.N. Division Royal Marine Light Infantry. Died 28 April 1917, aged 40. Buried Aubigny Communal Cemetery Extension. Pas de Calais, France. Bay 1. Son of Frederick & Cordella Farmer of Rose Tree Cottages, Bristol Road, Quedgeley. Husband of Ethel. M. Farmer, of 6 Victoria Cottages, Elmore Lane, Quedgeley, Gloucester.

A. J. Freeman. Private.A.J.31414. 2nd/5thBn. Gloucestershire Regiment. Died 28 June 1918, aged 19. Buried Berlin South-Western Cemetery. V.B.8. Son of Mr & Mrs A. Freeman of Elmore Lane, Quedgeley, Gloucester.

Arthur Moss Lovell. Lance Corporal 17164. 12th Bn. Gloucestershire Regiment. Died 23 August 1918, aged 23. Son of Henry & Rosa Jane Lovell of Severn Farm, Elmore Back, Gloucester. Buried Queens Cemetery, Bucquoy, Pas de Calais, France. Grave 1V. A. 7. Location. Bucquoy is situated on the D919, Arras-Amiens Road, 15 km south of Arras. Queens Cemetery is located on the western side of the road just south of the village of Bucquoy.

Charles Frederick Maycock. Private 26178 12 Bn. Gloucestershire Regiment. Died Thursday, 4 October 1917, aged 22. Remembered at the Tyne Cot Memorial,

Zonnebeke, West-Vlaanderen, Belgium. Panel 72-75. Son of Mrs Scotford of Quedgeley, Gloucester.

Edwin. J. Mortimer. Lance Sergeant 17045. 1st Bn. Grenadier Guards. Died Sunday, 17 September 1916. Buried Bronfay Farm Military Cemetery, Bray-Sur-Somme, Somme, France. Grave II.C.33.

Stanley Nash. Private 2410-37 2/1 Oxford & Bucks Light Infantry. Died 22 August 1917. Buried Tyne Cot Cemetery, Zonnebeke, West Vlaanderen, Belgium. Grave Panel 96-98.

Donald Humphrey Sessions MC. Lieutenant. No 2. School of Aerial Gunnery, Royal Air Force. Died Thursday 20 June 1918. Buried St. James' Church Yard, Quedgeley, Gloucester.

Henry Smith. Sergeant 8442 1st Bn. Gloucestershire Regiment. Died Tuesday, 22 August 1918. Remembered at the Thiepval Memorial. Somme, France. Pier and Face 5A and 5B.

Harry Leonard Squibbs. Sergeant 10649. The Wiltshire Regiment. Died 28 July 1920, aged 29. Buried at Quedgeley Churchyard, Gloucester. Son of William & Rosina Squibb of Dorchester, Dorset.

Charles George Townsend. PO/1763(S) 1st R.M. Bn. R.N. Div., Royal Marine Light Infantry. Died Tuesday, 6 November 1917. Remembered at the Tyne Cot Memorial, Zonnebeke, West-Vlaanderen, Belgium. Panel 1 & 162A.

Reginald George Stanley Veal. Corporal 2740 "C" Sqdn, 5th (Royal Irish) Lancers. Died Sunday, 1 November 1914, aged 22. Buried Boulogne Eastern Cemetery, Pas de Calais, France. Grave number III.B.21, Son of John Henry Charles & Sarah Veal, of Victoria Inn, Hucclecote, Gloucester.

The Roll of Honour for World War II (1939-1945)

Sidney Charles Biggs. Sergeant 1164957 11 Sqdn. Royal Air Force Volunteer Reserve. Died on Monday, 19 March 1945, aged 24. Buried Singapore Memorial Singapore. Grave or Reference Panel number Column 451. Son of Charles Daniel & ALICE Biggs of Hardwicke, Gloucester.

Frederick William Boughton. Sergeant 787160. The Royal Artillery. Died 20 May 1940, aged 30. Buried at the Warhem Military Cemetery. Pas de Calais, France. Row A. Grave 28.

Maurice Frank James Boulton. Sergeant Pilot 1380537 Royal Air Force Volunteer Reserve. Died 12 December 1941, aged 26. Buried Gibraltar (North Front) Cemetery, Gibraltar. Grave or Reference Panel Number Plot 2. Row A. Joint grave 12. Son of

Edward M. & Florence E. Boulton of Quedgeley, Gloucester.

David Hadley Morgan. Private 5184888. 5th Bn. Gloucestershire Regiment. Died Tuesday, 28 May 1940, aged 24. Remembered at Dunkirk Memorial Nord, France. Grave or Reference Panel Number. Column 57. Son of Alfred Edward & Mary Emily Morgan of Quedgeley.

Eric Bradley Potter. Sergeant 1585887. 90 Sqdn. Royal Air Force Volunteer Reserve. Died Wednesday, 14 July 1943. Buried at Heverlee War Cemetery. LEUVEN, Vlaams-Brabant, Belgium. Grave Number 5.A.13.

Howard Smith. Leading Aircraftman 1660333. Royal Air Force Volunteer Reserve. Died 17 February 1945. Buried at St. James' Church, Quedgeley, Gloucester, West of Church Tower.

Howard Charles Turner. Private 14716605 5/7th Bn. Gordon Highlanders. Died 25 October 1944, aged 24. Buried at the Bergen -OP -Zoom War Cemetery, Noord-Brabant, Netherlands. Grave or Reference Panel Number 12.B.6. Son of Sidney & May Turner and husband of Marjorie Turner, of Quedgeley, Gloucester.

Frederick Charles Turner. Private 14680138 5/7th Gordon Highlanders. Died 12 February 1945, aged 20. Buried at the Milsbeek War Cemetery, Limburg, Netherlands. Grave Number II.G.6. Son of Richard & Edith Turner of Burgess Hill, Sussex.

Past Church Ministers

Walter 1210	Adam 1269	Walshe 1329
Danyel 1469	(Sir) Robert 1493	J. Evans 1549
J. Bryan 1552	W. Gravestoke 1565	T. Wilcoxe 1585
J. Jenyns 1588	J. Hurdman 1650	G. Wall 1662
J. Makepeace 1662	T. Jowling 1712	P. Bons 1713
Jauncey 1770	J. Forthlock 1777	C. Palmer 1813
W. Foster 1818	R. Jones 1819	C. Hardwick 1822
J. Lee 1835	J. Headlam 1837	J. Russell 1838
T. Bowman 1838	E. Knollys 1842	F. Alley 1860
A. Bazett 1862	A. Nash 1876	E. Bryans 1890
S. Cornish 1896	F. Grenside 1907	E. Bartleet 1917
H. Hadow 1925	G. Harvey 1941	F. Lanham 1947
P. Dack 1962	G Stickland 1982	J. Ward 2012
M. Siddall 2022		

An Old Marriage Register

The Gloucestershire Genealogy website[1] lists the marriages at this Church between 1559 and 1836. A subset of the marriage registers from 1804 to 1836 is shown below.

George Vaile & Charlotte Tippin	19 Nov 1804
George Clifford & Mary Goodman	12 Jan 1807
John Taylor & Elizabeth Copner	23 Feb 1807
Thomas Stephens & Ann Drew	4 May 1807
Daniel Baker of Stonehouse & Mary Edge	26 Dec 1807
John Griffith & Hannah Ridler	10 Oct 1808
William Miles & Ann Cole	5 July 1809
Isaac Bevan & Mary Ely	5 Oct 1809
Thomas Butler of Trellock, Monmouth, & Susanna Beach	25 June 1811
Wm. Smith of Awre, Gloucs. & Mary Pride	19 Sept 1811
John Hawkins of Churcham & Sarah Copner	14 Apr 1812
Richard King of Kempsford, Gloucs. & Elizabeth Beach	23 June 1812
William Hill Burrup & Eleanor Ebborn of English Bicknor	29 Sept 1812
William Robertson & Hannah Phipps	22 Feb 1813
Richd. Witts of Sandhurst & Esther Brown	1 Feb 1814
William Strain of St. Mary de Lode, Gloster & Susanna Broban	27 July 1814
Thomas Ashby & Sarah Leech	12 Oct 1815
William Beach & Ann Guilding	5 Dec 1815
William Pride & Ann Hill	13 Dec 1815
William Cox & Ann Clifford	28 Mar 1816
Jno. Twinning of Badgeworth & Hester Priday	14 Oct 1816
James Slatter of St. Catherine's, Gloster, & Ann Beach	25 Nov 1816
John Clifford & Mary Ann Roberts	25 Jan 1817
Joseph Pegler & Sarah Dedge	29 Jan 1818
Jno. Merrett of Hardwicke & Sarah Ravenhill	9 Apr 1818
William Weeks & Hannah Richardson	15 June 1818
William Field & Sarah Cook of Berkeley	18 Mar 1819
John Carter of Elmore & Hester Harris	8 Apr 1819
Thomas Harris & Hannah Hems	28 Apr 1819
John Cale of Minsterworth & Sarah Fowler	27 May 1819

[1] See https://www.glosgen.co.uk/records/quedgeley.htm.

Chapter 4 – Our Buildings

Nath. Ratcliff of Woodchester & Mary Baker	23 Mar 1820
Charles James of Newnham, Gloucs., & Elizabeth Priday	27 June 1820
Henry Hawkins of Standish & Elizabeth Priday	4 Jan 1821
Wm. Kendall of Bradford, Wilts, & Ann Priday	11 Sept 1821
John Phelps of Hardwicke & Elizabeth Guilding	9 Apr 1822
George White & Hannah Powell, of the South Hamlet	20 May 1822
William Harris & Anne Turner	20 Sept 1822
Nathaniel Priday & Hester Hill	9 Apr 1823
Charles Harris & Elizabeth Brabant	5 Aug 1823
George Berrow of Frampton-on-Severn & Ann Gough	18 Oct 1823
Thomas Smith of Matson & Emma Priday	8 Jan 1824
Stephen Millard of St. Mary de Grace, Gloucester, & Jane Guilding	4 July 1825
George White & Rosannah Hawkins	3 Oct 1825
Harry Nisbet of Walcot, Bath & Anne Curtis-Hayward	19 Feb 1828
Thomas Taylor & Mary Ravenhill	4 Mar 1828
William Prien & Maria Dutfield	28 Oct 1828
Shad. Copner of Hardwicke & Martha Nash	10 May 1829
Joseph Hayes & Eliza Hawkins	3 July 1831
John Ridler & Ann Nash	6 Nov 1831
Charles Harris & Sarah Arch	8 Nov 1831
Joseph Priday & Rebecca Price	7 Feb 1832
Henry Beach of Randwick & Elizabeth Bailey	19 Apr 1832
Horatio Nelson Hawkins of Totteridge, Herts. & Sarah Bailey	5 June 1832
Thomas Priday & Elizabeth Heyden	24 Dec 1832
John Smith & Mary Boswell	24 May 1834
Samuel Winfield of Elmore & Anne Lane	20 Oct 1834
Charles Cole & Margaret Ford	29 Oct 1835
Joseph Taylor & Hetty Fisher of Littleworth	17 Mar 1836
James Hamlet of Hardwicke & Judith Ruck	17 May 1836
Thomas Perry of Upton St. Leonard's & Sarah Avery	3 July 1836
Thomas Hayes & Susan Ravenhill	12 Sept 1836
Richard Priday & Pamela Haven	17 Oct 1836
Wm. Green of Elmore & Elizabeth Bullock	27 Oct 1836
William Hill of Barton St. Mary, Gloucester & Jane Mercer	27 Nov 1836

An Early Church Parish Magazine

An early example of the monthly Church Parish Magazine for January 1906 may be found in Appendix A – 1906 Quedgeley Parish Magazine at the back of this book. In addition, I intend to donate a book called 'The Dawn of Day' (SPCK) which includes the monthly magazines for the whole of 1898 to the Gloucestershire Archives[2].

An Early Description of the Church

During his time as Rector, Revd Hadow (1925 to 1941) wrote some historical notes about the Church which we have reproduced in Appendix B – Church Notes by Revd H Hadow. Revd Hadow can be seen second from the right in Figure 40, along with three young choristers believed to be Master Brown on the far left, Master Morgan next to him and Master Wixey on the far right.

++++++++++++

Figure 40 – Revd Hadow with a few of the choir

The Rectory

Formerly a detached Victorian Rectory, it was built next to St James' Church in 1840 and became a Grade II listed building in 1985. The architect was Francis Niblett of Haresfield Court (1814 to 1883) and the builder, Edward Cholertons, with sons John, Robert and James. It was built with ashlar stone in a symmetrical Cotswold style.

The Rectory was a three-storey house with three reception rooms, five bedrooms and

---

[2] See https://www.gloucestershire.gov.uk/archives/.

four secondary attic bedrooms, a cellar, large garden and out-buildings.

Figure 41 – The Rectory

The Rectory was extended soon after it was built, then somewhat reduced in the 1960s. It was a fine home for Rectors over the decades. In the early years many housemaids served in the The Rectory, see Figure 42. Lucy Meadows was the house keeper, see Figure 43 (on page 50). The open fire grates in every room kept them busy carrying buckets of coal up the stairs.

Figure 42 – The Rectory Housemaids

Figure 43 – Housekeeper Lucy Meadows with husband Thomas, circa 1938

The Rectory was a village meeting place for the young and old. Many plays and fêtes were held on the front lawn in the summer and they were well-supported.

Figure 44 – A Play performed on The Rectory lawn

During the War years not a lot of work was done to the property. The cost to refurbish it was huge. The Revd F J Lanham was Rector from 1947 and in 1961 a Christian Stewardship Campaign was arranged. The St James' Church Parochial Church Council and helpers worked hard to recruit new planned giving supporters to help with the church's finances. A free supper was put on at RAF Quedgeley and a professional company came to talk to the guests. It was a great success.

Revd Paul Dack arrived with his mother in 1962 and swift changes were brought about. Land owned by the church nearby was sold to the Gloucester Rural District Council, to build bungalows for local pensioners. With the sale money, work could now start on The Rectory. It was rewired, central heating installed and decorated throughout. A two-story servants' north wing was knocked down and the car park was enlarged. The Revd Paul Dack transformed the garden with shrubs and trees and he tidied the churchyard.

Twenty years later, in 1982, The United Benefice of Hardwicke, Quedgeley, Elmore and Longney was formed. Revd Paul Dack moved out and was in charge of the Benefice of Hasfield and surrounding parishes, north of Gloucester. The Diocese of Gloucester sold The Rectory at auction and my husband and I bought it as a private dwelling. It was now independent of St James' Church and from that point onwards known as The Old Rectory. A new four-bedroom Rectory was built in the Old Rectory's kitchen garden, adjacent to St James' Church. Soon afterwards, The Revd Geoffrey Stickland and his family moved out of the nearby Hardwicke Vicarage into the new Quedgeley Rectory. The Hardwicke Vicarage was sold in 1983.

Page 52 — Memories of Quedgeley Gloucestershire

Figure 45 – The Rectory at the time it was sold

Figure 46 – My husband and I were the first private owners of The Old Rectory

Quedgeley Estates

The Manor

Durand was Sheriff of Gloucester in 1086. His nephew was Walter of Gloucester and he held Quedgeley in 1095. Quedgeley was passed onto Walter's son, Miles of Gloucester, Earl of Hereford. Later, Miles had two married daughters, Margaret and Lucy. Their husbands jointly owned The Manor at Quedgeley, east of Bristol Road. It was a twelfth century Manor, surrounded by a moat. When the time came, Margaret passed her share of The Manor onto Llanthony Priory, Gloucester.

In 1137 it was said the tithes of The Manor mill were granted to Llanthony Priory. By 1146, The Manor at Quedgeley had fishponds as well as a moat. These tithes also went to the Priory. In 1359 The Priory complained that the fish had been stolen.

During 1524 The Prior of Llanthony held his Court in the room above the parlour, at The Manor. In 1535 King Henry VIII granted the Manor to John Mallet, which Arthur Porter held. Arthur's two daughters are mentioned on a brass plaque in St James' Church. In 1541, after the King's dissolution, Llanthony Priory, Gloucester, gave up the ownership of Quedgeley Manor and laid a Royal Charge upon the living, which was only released in 1928, by being bought out by the Ecclesiastical Commissioners.

The Water Mill, near Long Field, was farmed by The Manor. By 1565, William Doddington was at The Manor. By 1600, William's son held The Manor. He died in 1638 and The Manor should have passed to his son, William. Sadly, William passed his sword through his mother's body and killed her. He could not inherit and it passed onto his brother John. Son-in-law Thomas Hoby sold The Manor onto Henry Chapman in 1692. Thomas and Elizabeth Whorwood were there in 1717. By 1736 John Yate of Arlingham had bought The Manor.

The Manor in 1800 was now owned by John Beach of Hardwicke. It passed onto Colonel John Curtis-Hayward in 1867. His maiden aunts lived there until the end of the nineteenth century.

The Government purchased most of the land in 1915 to build the National Filling Factory No. 5. Around the Manor house and surrounding area, land was used for a Cavalry Depot. After World War I, The Manor Farm became a Ploughing School for ex-service men (See Figure 47, page 54) and the surplus land was let to three farmers, Mr Phipps, Captain Clarke and Mr Hazel.

Figure 47 – Wounded soldiers retraining at The Manor

By 1924 the National Filling Factory had been dismantled. In 1939 the Secretary of State for Air Ministry acquired land at Manor Farm from Gloucestershire County Council to build the RAF Maintenance Unit, Quedgeley. Surplus land was now rented by the Phipps family and the Brooks family. The Manor Farmhouse was divided into two. They farmed the land for many years. The Manor still stands, extensively modernised, and is now situated in the area known as Kingsway, on the east side of the A38 Quedgeley by-pass.

Woolstrop Manor

In the hamlet of Dudstone and Kings Barton, west of Quedgeley Church, Robert de Pontlarge at his death in or before 1246, held Woolstrop. He passed Woolstrop to his son William. William granted Woolstrop Manor sometime before 1252 to William de Valence, Earl of Pembroke. The Earl also owned Moreton Valence Manor, Gloucester.

By the thirteenth century the Walsh family were Lords of the Manor at Woolstrop. This family also farmed land at Netheridge, north of Quedgeley. They held both estates until the sixteenth century. George Kenn sold Woolstrop to William Hayward, who had died by 1696. Woolstrop stayed with the Hayward family and in the late eighteenth century they built a large new family home north-west of Woolstrop Manor and called it Quedgeley House. It was a two-storied building of ashlar, with an overhanging slate roof. It had a porch which was later demolished. The house was later enlarged on the west side. In 1818 Albinia Frances Hayward became the owner and later married the Revd John Adey Curtis and added his name to her family name.

At the entrance, on the Longney Road (now School Lane), stood a small lodge which housed the Manor's coachman and his family. Once through the gate, there was a long drive through the tree-lined park to the house.

Figure 48 – Woolstrop Lodge

Mrs A F Curtis-Hayward died in 1860 and her son Colonel John Curtis-Hayward became owner of Quedgeley House. He died in 1874 and the estate passed to his son John Frederick Curtis-Hayward who died in 1924. He was Quedgeley Parish Council Chairman for 30 years. The last family member to own the estate was John Frederick's nephew Reginald. The estate was sold in lots in 1939.

Many years later Glevum builders bought Quedgeley House with land and Woolstrop Farm.

In the middle of the twentieth century Quedgeley House was converted into 12 flats. In the 1980s Quedgeley House was demolished and hundreds of houses were built on the land.

A punctual attendance is requested as the Sale will commence precisely at the time stated

By Direction of The Hesketh Estates, Ltd.

THE QUEDGELEY HOUSE ESTATE
QUEDGELEY, near GLOUCESTER
Within 3 miles of the City centre, on the main Bristol Road, comprising:

QUEDGELEY HOUSE

21 bed and dressing rooms, 4 bathrooms, 4 reception rooms, etc. (at present requisitioned).

Secondary Residence known as WOOLSTROP COTTAGE

3 Attractive Farms of 236 acres, 99 acres and 55 acres. Cottages. About 90 ACRES are scheduled for development with the lay-out approved and passed by the local authority. All main services. The whole extending to about 417 ACRES and producing £1,120 gross p.a.

For SALE by AUCTION as a WHOLE or in LOTS
Solicitors: Messrs. SLAUGHTER & MAY, 18, Austin Friars, E.C.2., Particulars (in course of preparation) may be had when ready from the Auction HAMPTON & SONS. LTD., 6, Arlington Street, S.W.1. (Tel.: REG. 822

CATALOGUE.

FIRST DAY'S SALE

ON TUESDAY, 27 JUNE, 1939

Purchasers are requested to make use of this slip in giving their Names and Addresses to the Auctioneers.

Purchaser's Name ....

Address in full..

BRUTON, KNOWLES & CO.,

Figure 49 – The Auction of Quedgeley House Estate in 1939

Chapter 4 – Our Buildings   Page 57

QUEDGELEY HOUSE
QUEDGELEY

Within 3 miles of Gloucester and near to the main Bristol Road

---

CATALOGUE
OF A PORTION OF THE

VALUABLE FURNITURE
AND EFFECTS
including

Old Oak Chests, Dresser, Cupboard, and Monks' Bench.
Queen Anne Musical and Chiming Clock in green lacquer case,
and other pieces of the same period.
Chippendale Carved Mirror and Brackets, Kneehole Table,
and Serpentine Commode.
Sheraton Card Tables, Pembroke and Sofa Tables,
and Pair of Side Tables.
8ft. Mahogany Sideboard, Dining Table in three divisions,
Set of Sixteen Chairs, Steck Pianola Piano,
Two Axminster Carpets, 6ft. 6in. Mahogany Wardrobe.
Old English and Chinese Porcelain, Pictures,
Blunderbuss and Pistols with silver mounts.
B·T·H Electric Refrigerator, Belling Cooker.
WOLSELEY "SALON DE VILLE" MOTOR CAR, 1937
Austin 12-h.p. Truck,
Green's 20in. Motor Mower, Garden Tools,
108 Head of Poultry, Poultry Houses, etc.
Large Quantity of Greenhouse, Flowering, Decorative and
Bedding-out Plants

which

BRUTON, KNOWLES & CO.

Are instructed by Reginald Curtis-Hayward, Esq., for whom they have sold the Estate

TO SELL BY AUCTION

ON TUESDAY & WEDNESDAY, 27 & 28 JUNE, 1939
At Twelve o'clock each day

May be viewed Monday, 26 June, from 10 to 4
Catalogues may be had of the Auctioneers, Gloucester

W. Judd, Printer St. John's Lane, Gloucester

Figure 50 – Quedgeley House Estate Contents for auction in 1939

Figure 51 – Woolstrop Cottage on School Lane

Woolstrop Farm

This was known as the Home Farm. The entrance was via School Lane and along The Rectory Lane. At the end of the lane you met a five-barred gate, then you had arrived. The land lay between the Bristol Road in the east and the Gloucester & Sharpness Canal in the west. It was a mixed farm of crops and cattle. Louis E M Carter and his wife farmed there in the nineteenth century. In 1915 their son Cary, aged 20, was killed in World War I, see Figure 53 (on page 59). Later, their son Leonard and his wife Alice took on the tenancy from Quedgeley House and ran the farm with their three daughters. In 1939 Quedgeley House, Woolstrop Cottage and Woolstrop Farm were split up and sold. Leonard Carter bought his farm and the family stayed there until they were bought out in 1960 by Glevum Builders. The farmhouse and land were let for many years. Eventually the builders got planning permission to develop. Today in its place we have the Tesco superstore and petrol station, library, health centre, two doctor's surgeries, dentist, police station, junior school and hundreds of homes on the land beyond, towards the canal.

Figure 52 – Woolstrop Farm

Figure 53 – Cary Carter from Woolstrop Farm

Field Court Estate

This estate, once in Hardwicke, consisted of 130 acres of farmland and was transferred to Quedgeley in 1935.

In 1185 little is known of William Clinton, Earl of Hungtingdon, who held Field Court Manor, Hardwicke. By 1307 Robert de la Field was the owner in the reign of King Edward II, until 1327. It was a large estate, east of Quedgeley Church, with a black and white timbered house and a moat.

In 1505 Thomas, son of John Deerhurst MP, died and left Field Court to his wife, Mary, who died in 1510. Richard Barrow was living at Field Court in the early sixteenth century, but they were not welcomed at St James' Church by Arthur Porter of the Manor Estate. In 1642 Colonel John Barrow was at Field Court at the time of the Civil War, and by 1651 the Parliamentarians won, with 100,000 men killed.

By the early eighteenth century we hear the South Aisle at St James' Church belonged to the Barrow Family of Field Court. The dispute had been sorted. The estate changed ownership several times and was farmed successfully. By the 1930s Field Court had passed from the Mills family to Colonel John Curtis-Hayward. John Cole was the last farmer and he sold Field Court Estate to Robert Hitchens, Builders, in the 1960s, see Figure 54 (on page 60). Hundreds of houses were built in the 1970s. The main farmhouse was rebuilt and 27 retirement homes added nearby.

Figure 54 – Field Court Farm pre-1970

Netheridge Estate

Netheridge was Quedgeley's most northern estate, by the River Severn, almost in Gloucester. Nicholas Avenell was living there in 1219 and Robert Avenell then gave Netheridge to Hugh of Kingsholm, Gloucester. By 1255 Hugh had passed Netheridge onto Adam de Valence. It was now the property of Llanthony Priory, Gloucester. Twenty years later the Walsh Family were the owners and remained there until the sixteenth century. They also had other land in Quedgeley. Jasper Selwyn took over Netheridge in 1605. John Beach of Quedgeley Manor held the estate before the end of the eighteenth century. By 1841 Netheridge had left Quedgeley Parish and was a part of Hempsted. In 1846 William Beach sold Netheridge to Samuel Lysons. In 1899 Mrs G S Lysons sold Netheridge to Major J D Birchall of Upton St Leonards, Gloucester. Major J D Birchall's representatives then sold out to Gloucester Corporation in 1943. They built Gloucester's sewage-pumping station and treatment plant, which was working by 1963. The odour at nearby Quedgeley was terrible for many years. The seventeenth century farmhouse and remaining land continued to be farmed by Claire and Daniel Lovell and their son Kenneth. The farm ceased before the end of the twentieth century. Most of the land has now been developed and has the southwest bypass running through it.

The National Filling Factory No. 5

In October 1915 building started on the National Filling Factory No. 5, on the north side of Naas Lane. It was set up by the Ministry of Munitions, under Prime Minister David Lloyd-George. It was one of four Quick Firing (QF) establishments in Britain as there was a shortage of shells needed for World War I. The site was on land at Manor Farm, owned by the Curtis-Hayward family of Quedgeley House. In quick time 250 wooden sheds were erected on 308 acres of the farm. The Midland Railway and the Great Western Railway mainlines ran east of the site. The Midland Railway provided a connection to the Shell Filling Station. This was to deliver goods and take away explosives and other essentials. The workers also used the line to come to work.

In June 1916 there were 2,113 women and 307 men on the books. A Munition worker's wage was £1 per week in 1916, and a third-class weekly return rail ticket

Chapter 4 – Our Buildings   Page 61

cost 2s 2d (11p) from either Cheltenham, Gloucester or Stroud. Many walked or cycled miles to work. Those who came into contact with explosives could be identified by their orange-yellow faces and hands, caused by TNT dust in the assembling rooms. The women were called Canary Girls. By March 1917 the factory had 5,644 women, 720 men on its books with WPC Marion Sandover in attendance (see Figure 56). By October 1918, there were 6,227 women.

Figure 55 – The Munitions 'Canary Girls'

With the end of World War I in November 1918, operations at the factory quickly came to a halt. The shell fillers were demobilised, having done their bit. Over 10,500,000 shells were filled and assembled, along with 7,000,000 cartridges and 23,500,000 fuses and other components, and the finished ammunition had been despatched by rail to the south coastal ports.

WPC Sandover c.1917

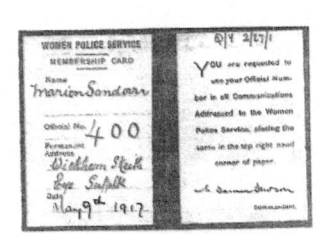

Marion Sandover's Warrant Card

Constable Sandover was supplied by the Women's Auxiliary Service to serve as Policewoman in the munitions factory at Quedgeley during the Great War, and was appointed to Gloucestershire Constabulary in 1918.

from *The Policewoman's Review* 1935

Figure 56 – WPC Marion Sandover

RAF Quedgeley

In 1938 Prime Minister Neville Chamberlain started preparations to increase Britain's military capability for defence, as the threat of war was becoming extremely likely. Germany was now turning its eyes to countries closer to home.

The Manor Farm was chosen as a suitable site to build a maintenance unit. It would be called 'The RAF Equipment Storage Depot and Vehicle Park, No. 7 Maintenance Unit'. It was on the same site that the National Filling Station No. 5 had stood during World War I. Building started in 1938 and the unit was officially opened on 15 April 1939. The maintenance unit had its Headquarters in Naas Lane and seven other local sites. It comprised a total of 525 acres of land and 2,000,000 square feet of storage, all within four miles, south of Gloucester off the Bristol Road. The Mechanical Transport Section was set up. The task was to store vehicles which would eventually be wanted overseas in the event of war. When the vehicles arrived at Quedgeley they had the petrol, water, batteries and tools removed and stored in the sheds. The RAF had so many vehicles that Kingscote Park Dursley, Haresfield Court and Hardwicke Court all had to help store them, mainly outside. The depot was operating all day, every day. American and British aircraft spares, clothing, fabric, paint, ground equipment, parachutes, gun turrets, weapons and medical items were also stored at the No. 7 Maintenance Unit.

During September 1940 Canadian-born Flight Lieutenant Robert Coventry, aged 27, was in control of a Bristol Blenheim bomber. Together with two crew mates, they were on a simulated bombing mission off the Welsh coast. As they made their way back to their base in Cambridgeshire, they had engine failure over Gloucestershire. The pilot landed in Quedgeley, very close to the Church of England School. The pilot was killed but the two crew members survived.

Figure 57 – Flight Lieutenant Robert Coventry

Chapter 4 – Our Buildings	Page 63

In 1940, the Worcester Regiment provided the guards at No. 7 Maintenance Unit and they were billeted on site. The Gloucester Regiment, the Air Ministry Constabulary and the RAF Regiment also served time at the Unit. When the RAF Regiment moved out, the Polish Army arrived. They were superseded by German Prisoners of War. Later, 270 Italian Prisoners of War were stationed at Quedgeley Court, in the north of Quedgeley, and were brought in every day by vehicles to work at the depot. There were 1,118 service officers, non-commissioned officers and airmen, plus 3,400 civilians working at the unit at the height of the War. The busiest time was the run-up to D-Day on 6 June 1944.

A Spitfire aircraft crashed into a storage shed at No. 6 Site, killing the pilot and a local young woman named Etta Jelf. The only other tragedy was in 1949 when the Commanding Officer, Group Captain Reed, committed suicide in his room in the officers' mess and was given a military funeral at St James' Church, Quedgeley.

The employees were entertained by the National Services Association and Workers Playtime during the lunch breaks in the headquarter's canteen. In the mornings and afternoons tea came around in a white enamel bucket at one old penny per cup.

From time to time well-known people toured around No. 7 Maintenance Unit and its sites. Her Majesty Queen Mary made a visit in 1941. She stayed at Badminton House, Gloucestershire, for some time during the War.

Figure 58 – Queen Mary's visit to RAF Quedgeley in 1941

The Germans had a map of No. 7 Maintenance Unit and they knew it had important War supplies there. They dropped a few explosives on their way to bomb Birmingham, but they did not do too much damage.

The RAF service men gradually departed, only sixty were left in 1948 and all had gone by 1950. The Air Ministry Constabulary then took over guarding all the sites. There were 70 constables, eight sergeants, one sub-inspector and the chief, also two resident CIB officers and two search women.

In 1955 32 houses were built on Ministry land. They were married quarters for the police. These quarters were named Needham Avenue, after Group Captain S W Needham, Station Commander from July 1956 to April 1959.

No. 7 Maintenance Unit carried on being a major equipment supply depot until 1965, then the Ministry of Defence had a change of policy and Quedgeley's big storage sheds were the home for 'Defence Accommodation Stores'. The Unit provided household goods for the Royal Navy, Army and RAF. All kinds of household furniture arrived which was mended and sent out to barracks, service hospitals and married quarters in this country and abroad. In 1967 RAF Quedgeley had 551 acres of land and employed 1,750 staff, mostly civilians.

In 1973 Sir Anthony Kershaw, MP for the Stroud Constituency from 1955 to 1987, asked why 17 RAF Houses in Needham Avenue, Quedgeley, had remained empty for almost a year. The Housing Manager from the Gloucester Rural District Council contacted the Ministry of Defence to see if the houses could be transferred to the Rural District Council and then let to local people. This was finally agreed.

With Local Government reorganisation in 1973/4, RAF Quedgeley came under the new Stroud District Council. On 14 February 1980, at a meeting held in the council chambers in John Street, Stroud, No. 7 Maintenance Unit was formally adopted. The council gave the RAF Quedgeley Commanding Officer permission to fly his official flag whenever he was present in any part of the district. A formal presentation was later held at Stratford Park Leisure Centre. My husband and I were invited and enjoyed the band concert.

In 1979 the Church was delighted to join the RAF in celebrating 40 years in Quedgeley, see Figure 59 (on page 65). The front row, from left to right, is Cllr Ken Meek, Nancy Stroud, Caroline Meek, Cllr Tony Stroud, Group Captain M J Allistone and his wife, and Revd F J Lanham, Rector of St James' Church from 1947 to 1962.

Figure 59 – Celebrating 40 years of the RAF in Quedgeley, 1939-1979

At the time of the Falklands Conflict in April 1982, No. 7 Maintenance Unit was rushed off its feet supplying Defence Accommodation Stores for 200 warships, and subsequently for all the ground forces sent to recover the Islands.

A cost-saving exercise took place and RCA and Securicor won the contract to manage looking after the Defence Accommodation Stores from 1984. Three hundred employees were made redundant at the unit. Both new companies promised to find work for 200 employees. The new employer's name was changed later to Serco. The RAF unit won back the contract in 1990.

The First Gulf War was starting in 1990 and by early January 1991 coalition forces, including British troops, began their attack on Iraq by sea and air. Iraq was invading their Kuwait neighbours. It was all over by the end of 28 February 1991. RAF Quedgeley played a big part, sending out stretchers, wheelchairs and other equipment.

Finally, help was provided in the former Republic of Yugoslavia. The country was divided into independent States in the 1990s. It did not work out and Christians were fighting with Muslims. The United Nations Peace Force intervened with the support from RAF Quedgeley; help was given to the troops and aid to the civil community. Between 1992 and 1995 Quedgeley sent out large lorries to Bosnia, to help with the despatching of stores.

The number of civilians left working at No. 7 Maintenance Unit and the seven sites dropped from 600 in the early 1990s to 250 in 1995. Gradually the land was sold for businesses and housing estates. The first land to be sold, in 1995, was 24 acres at RAF No. 3 Site, Elmore Lane. Warehouses were being let at the Headquarters. The decision was made to close the unit on 31 March 1996.

The last Commander, Group Captain Peter P Gaskin OBE, invited (through the local Gloucester Citizen Newspaper) all current and ex-employees of RAF Quedgeley and their partners to attend the formal closure parade, fly-past and lunch on 15 March 1996. The parade was to start at 10:15am, with over 600 attending on that special day.

Figure 60 – The closing of RAF Quedgeley: Formal Closure Lunch

Unfortunately, thick cloud and drizzle meant a fly-past by three C-130 Hercules transport aircraft from RAF Lyneham had to be cancelled. The stirring tones of the marching music from the band of the RAF Regiment made up for it.

Figure 61 – The closing of RAF Quedgeley: Band of the RAF Regiment

Chapter 4 – Our Buildings   Page 67

The Service of Commemoration was led by The Revd Geoffrey Stickland, Rector of St James' Church, Quedgeley, and Unit Chaplain. The Revd Group Captain Ted Hill, from nearby RAF Innsworth Unit in Gloucester, also officiated. Prayers were said and hymns were sung. In Figure 62, we can see Flying Officer Lynne Ploutarchou, Air Vice Marshall Richard Kyle, Ken Gleed, Group Captain Peter Gaskin, Revd Group Captain Ted Hill and Revd Geoffrey Stickland at the service.

Figure 62 – The closing of RAF Quedgeley: Service of Commemoration

The Sunset Ceremony took place, even though it was only 11:00am. The Ensign was brought down to the sound of the Last Post, played by the buglers from the RAF, Army and Navy, see Figure 63 (on page 68). The Ensign was then given to Revd Geoffrey Stickland for safe keeping. The Ensign was later formally hung in St James' Church.

Air Vice Marshall Richard Kyle, Air Officer Commanding Maintenance Units, reflected on the station's history. Quedgeley's longest-serving member of the civilian staff, Ken Gleed, recalled his fondest memories. After the ceremony the guests walked to the nearby hanger for a buffet lunch and enjoyed meeting with old friends and colleagues.

The unit was officially closed and put under the command of No. 16 Maintenance Unit RAF Stafford on 1 April 1997. It was the end of over 87 years of loyal service by the people of Quedgeley and District, for both War efforts.

In January 2000 developers revealed plans for an urban village, with 2,650 homes on the old RAF site. The builders contributed £6,000,000 towards the new southwest bypass. In October 2004 the site was formally renamed Kingsway. Quedgeley residents were not happy because they had voted to call the new area Manor Farm.

Figure 63 – The closing of RAF Quedgeley: Lowering the Ensign

Chapter 4 – Our Buildings   Page 69

Over the many years there had been a good social contact between the RAF and the local people. The Commanding Officer would invite the Quedgeley Parish Council Chairman and partner to the RAF Annual Party at the Headquarters (see Figure 64), together with other Councillors from Stroud District Council. Also, all the Quedgeley Parish Councillors were invited for a tour of the unit and then they were provided with a lunch in the officers' mess.

Figure 64 – RAF Quedgeley Annual Party in 1980

Many local boys joined Number 2419 (Quedgeley) Squadron Air Training Corps founded in 1944. Many years later their headquarters was in a building on No. 3 Site, Elmore Lane, Quedgeley. Parade evenings were on Mondays and Thursdays, 7:00pm to 9:00pm. The Air Cadets enjoyed an Annual Camp, which was usually a week at an RAF Camp.

The RAF Officers always came to St James' Church for the Sunday Service closest to 15 September each year which was the day in 1940 when Britain's airmen downed 186 German planes, the highest tally during the Battle of Britain. The last Battle of Britain Service was in September 1995 and was conducted by The Revd Geoffrey Stickland. The RAF officers also came to the November Remembrance Services held at the church, and laid a wreath at the War Memorial, together with an act of remembrance.

The RAF Quedgeley Fire and Rescue Service were well-known when they attended fêtes and garden parties locally. The firemen collected for many charities, including £1,500 in 1989 for the Children in Need Appeal. The RAF Quedgeley Charitable Appeals & Fundraising Committee put on a day to remember on 5 August 1989. It was the Unit's Fiftieth Anniversary Open Day. They raised thousands of pounds for five charities. The last RAF Summer Fayre was held in June 1995 and their final fireworks display was in November the same year, when 2,000 people attended.

Over the 57 years history, RAF Quedgeley provided 13 Guide Dogs for the Blind and raised over £100,000. The very last successful car boot sale held in December 1995 made thousands, and in 1996 £15,800 was donated to local Charities. Well done RAF Quedgeley, we all miss you!

Quedgeley Village Hall

It was 1928 when Mrs Tidswell opened the new Quedgeley Village Hall. Figure 65 shows some of the guests: (left to right) Sir Lionel Darrell and Lady Darrell and Mr Arch. On the doorstep holding programmes we have Reginald Curtis-Hayward and his wife, Evan Vaile and Mrs Mayo. On the far right we have George Wixey.

Figure 65 – The opening of The First Quedgeley Village Hall in 1928

The Village Hall had been built on land that had been given by the Curtis-Hayward family. The site was near the main Bristol Road and it had a car park on the front of the building. It was a single storey brick-built building, with an entrance porch leading into one large Hall. There was a big stage at the far end of the Hall, and doors either side, leading to the rear kitchen and toilets. George Wixey built the Hall and it cost £685. It was the only Village Hall locally. Other villages still used their schools for meetings.

A committee was formed comprising Mr R C Butt (Chairman) and members Mr A E Morgan, Mr Leah (architect), Miss J Curtis-Hayward, Reginald Curtis-Hayward, Miles Curtis-Hayward, Mr W J George, Cecil Morse, Leonard Carter, Mr C Harris, Evan Vaile, Revd H Hadow, Miss Powell and Mrs Mayo.

Soon Quedgeley had an Amateur Dramatic Society. Olive and Marjorie Parsons made many of the costumes. The Hall stayed open throughout World War II. Socials were held and raised money for the serving soldiers. In 1942 twenty Committee Members were elected at the Quedgeley Village Hall's AGM. My father was a member and one of the trustees.

In the early 1950s Harry Gage brought his projector along and put on a weekly film show for the younger generation. The Quedgeley & District Youth Club met each week and held regular dances. Whist drives were always popular on Thursdays.

My late husband Ken went onto the Village Hall committee in 1957 and continued to serve on the new Village Hall committee. He finally retired in 1995.

After the fire in 1958 with four years of fundraising and a grant, a new Hall was built in 1962. The second Village Hall was opened by Miles Curtis-Hayward on 17 February 1962, see Figure 66 (on page 72) and Figure 67 (on page 73). In Figure 68 (on page 73), we see the four Trustees (left to right): Cyril Mayo, Herbert Ely, Miles Curtis-Hayward and Revd Paul Dack together with Mr Close, the Village Hall secretary. A large gathering enjoyed the ceremony and the party that followed. It was a completely different building but on the same site.

After the hall opened it was a hard job to get a booking. The hall had a wonderful wooden floor, which we would put shuffleboard wax on for the dances, see Figure 69 (on page 74). Stiletto heel shoes were not allowed and ladies had to buy heel caps for their shoes. All the past users came back after the break. In Figure 70 (on page 74), we can see the 1963 St James' Church harvest supper with helpers at the back (left to right): Fred Tranter, Ken Meek and Tom King.

Quedgeley was growing fast. The hall was modern and well-equipped for large and small functions. In the 1980s whist drives, dancing classes, Golden Age club, Karate instructions, Mother and Toddler Club, all had many members. By now the St James Centre in School Lane had opened its doors, followed by the new Youth and Community Centre, and many more clubs met there. By the 1990s Kung Fu, Tumble Tots, ballet classes, aerobics and short-mat bowling still met in the Quedgeley Village Hall. Today, it is still a popular, well-kept hall to meet in.

THE Quedgeley Village Hall

OFFICIAL OPENING

OF THE

NEW VILLAGE HALL

BY MILES CURTIS - HAYWARD, ESQ.

supported by

Major Birchall, Mr. A. E. Keys, Mr. W. R. Watkins
and others

will take place on

SATURDAY, FEBRUARY 17, 1962

at 3.0 p.m.

TO WHICH ALL RESIDENTS IN THE PARISH ARE CORDIALLY INVITED

Following the opening ceremony and the inspection of the premises refreshments will be served to the O.A.P. members of the parish

A VILLAGE SOCIAL EVENING

will be held from 7.0 p.m. to 11.0 p.m.

TO WHICH ALL PARISHIONERS ARE INVITED

Refreshments will be provided and admission will be FREE

Come and See YOUR NEW HALL and have an enjoyable afternoon and evening

The Committee regrets that the wearing of **Stiletto Heeled Shoes** must be **Strictly Prohibited** at all times in the New Hall in order to preserve the magnificent floors, and it is hoped that all ladies will co-operate fully with the Committee in this respect.

Figure 66 – The opening of The Second Quedgeley Village Hall in 1962

Chapter 4 – Our Buildings
Page 73

Figure 67 – The opening ceremony for the Second Quedgeley Village Hall

Figure 68 – The Trustees & Secretary for the Second Quedgeley Village Hall

Figure 69 – Old Time Dance in the Second Quedgeley Village Hall in 1968

Figure 70 – St James' Harvest Supper in the Second Quedgeley Village Hall, 1963

Youth and Community Centre

After the Quedgeley Church of England School closed in School Lane, the concrete buildings in the yard were used to provide rooms for meetings and clubs. The old school buildings became known as The St James Centre. The owners were St James' Church Parochial Church Council and the Gloucestershire County Council.

Figure 71 – The St James Centre

However, the residents were calling for a new Youth and Community Centre because the St James Centre and the Village Hall could not cater with all the bookings.

Time went by and St James Centre was reaching the end of its life. Mike King was in charge of the St James Centre Manpower Services Project and called a meeting in January 1987 to see if there was any interest in building a new centre.

A steering group was set up by St James' Church Parochial Church Council Treasurer to look into building a new Youth and Community Centre on the old church school site in School Lane.

The Parish Council became involved and in time came up with plans and the estimated cost could be between £800,000 and £1,000,000. The Parish Council voted in favour of borrowing up to £300,000, subject to the approval from the people living in the area. The Council was promised £200,000 from Gloucestershire County Council and nothing from Gloucester City Council.

Anne Balchin, Secretary to the St James Centre Sub-Committee and Treasurer of the St James' Church Parochial Church Council, insisted "*We must find out what the locals want first*" and called for a meeting to be held in the Village Hall. At the meeting on 23 March 1993, Mike King told the large gathering, "*This is a project for all the residents of Quedgeley, both old and new, to decide what community facilities they need and then to expect all the local representatives to work together to achieve this*".

Dancey and Meredith, Architects in Gloucester were chosen to draw up plans for a

Youth and Community Centre in 1993 and it was built over the next year, at a cost of over £500,000 which was to be paid for by the Quedgeley parish rate payers and grants.

Some people thought that an expensive new building was not needed, but work started on 25 July 1994 and was expected to take thirty-four weeks to complete. It would be a single-story building, with two large halls, a kitchen, a committee room and a bar. A large area of the building would be for the use of the local youth.

The Youth and Community Centre was opened at the beginning of August 1995 by Mary Hinder and Miss Marshall, see Figure 72 and Figure 73 (on page 77).

The Quedgeley Social Club Limited moved into rooms at the Centre. On 21/11/1997 the first Licensors were David Brearey, Graham Burch and Anne Balchin.

Quedgeley Community Trust ran the Centre initially then the Quedgeley Parish Council took it over on 1 July 1999.

It is a very popular and well-used Youth and Community Centre of which the residents are proud.

Figure 72 – The opening of the Youth and Community Centre in 1995

Figure 73 – Mrs Hinder & Miss Marshall open the Youth and Community Centre

Severnvale Shopping Centre

In the middle of the 1950s Quedgeley was still a small country village. From the 1970s onwards, new residential and industrial buildings started moving in fast. Provisions for shops had not been catered for and the residents were unhappy.

It was not until 1983 that Stroud District Council Planning Department passed plans for an £80,000,000 shopping centre, public house and 2,300 new homes.

Tesco

The first phase was to build a superstore on land near Bristol Road, next to the existing Village Hall. The owners, Robert Hitchens Ltd and Glevum Estate Group Ltd gave the building contract to Britannia (Cheltenham) and the architects were Peter Wolstenhulme & Partners.

The store was leased to Tesco and was a 3,000 square metre single-storey building with six attached small shops and a car park with 450 spaces. The building would take 42 weeks. Steel frames soon appeared on the site and the foundation stone was laid on 17 January 1984 by the Chairman of Stroud District Council, Cllr Roy Nicholas, see Figure 74 (on page 78). The Tesco Superstore opened on 18 September 1984.

Figure 74 – The laying of the Foundation Stone for Severnvale Shopping Centre

Two hundred and fifty new jobs were created and 125 staff came from the closed Gloucester Centre Tesco Store.

Public House

A public house in front of Tesco came next, for Banks Brewery of the Black Country. Barnwood Builders of Gloucester had the contract to build and the cost was almost £550,000. The Chairman of Banks laid the final ridge tile at the 'topping - out' ceremony on the roof in early March 1985 and the new building was called The Basket Maker after the skilled tradesmen of Quedgeley. Their memorabilia hung from the walls. Sadly, the premises name has now been changed to The Haywain.

Albert and Pat Dean welcomed their first customers on 9 May 1985.

Figure 75 – The Original Basket Maker Pub

Tesco Extension

Planning permission was given in December 1985 to extend the Tesco Superstore by a third from just over 3,000 square metres to 4,000 square metres at a cost of approximately £3,500,000. The plan includes a new children's clothing section, a coffee shop and a fish bar.

Also, plans were passed to build a library, health clinic, two doctors' surgeries, a dentist's surgery, a police station, a petrol station, Beeches Green's new primary school nearby, and 2,300 new homes. The homes could only be built after the other facilities were completed. The police station and the library would be built by the developers and then leased to the County Council. The health clinic and surgeries were matters for the Area Health Authority and the Family Practitioners Committee.

Library

The library's land was donated to the County Council by Quedgeley District Centre Ltd. The first turf was cut in May 1988. It took the builders Flewelling and Seeley 12 months to build and cost £249,000.

On 10 August 1989 the new L-shaped library was opened by Mike Skinner, Chairman of the County Recreation and Leisure Committee, with 100 guests.

Figure 76 – The opening of the Library in 1989

Health Centre

The building of the new Health Centre behind Tesco started on 27 January 1989 when the first turf was cut (see Figure 77) by Mr W L Oakes (known as Bill) and M/s Rennie Fitch. The buildings were to be completed by Spring 1990. The cost was approximately £714,000 with £300,000 coming from the NHS. Dr Brooke and Dr Calvert moved from The Chantry Surgery on Bristol Road. Dr Bailey, Dr Knight and Dr Paterson came from the Carters Orchard Surgery. Mr Matthewson brought his Dental Practice from the Holly Grove estate. Dr Duggal had a new doctor's surgery in School Lane and Mr Rees a Dental Practice on the Bristol Road.

Figure 77 – Cutting the first turf for the Health Centre

Police Station

The Police Station on the same site was a disappointment for many residents, as the doors were nearly always closed and the premises used as office space.

Methodist Church

The Methodist Church, in the Gloucester Circuit, is of brick, with courses of blue brick and has narrow pointed windows. It had an extension in 1989 and services were held in the Scouts' & Guides' Headquarters for a while. The Methodist Church has benefited from the growing population in the area and has been well-maintained.

Figure 78 – Beautiful hand-drawing of the Methodist Church

Figure 79 – Methodist Church Sunday School Outing, 1920s

Quedgeley Schools

The Early Schools

There is very little information regarding the early schools in Quedgeley. A Dame School existed in 1693 and another in 1763. The schools may have taught lessons in one of the Manors. The National Society, set up by the state in the early nineteenth century, promoted Church of England Education. The Society taught religion, literacy and numeracy. Quedgeley had two Dame Schools in 1818 and a Sunday School for 30 children. By 1853, the Sunday School had increased to 45 children and it was held in a building, provided by the Curtis-Hayward family, located east of St James' Church.

Figure 80 – The Sunday School (on the right), taken in 1938

The National School

In 1883 the new single-storey brick Victorian School (as it was known locally) was built at the top of School Lane. Mr Thomas Beacall became the Headmaster. Fees in state schools were abolished by 1891, and the leaving age was raised to 11 years of age. Attendance recorded at the Victorian School in 1904 was 114 children. By 1922 it had dropped to 80. They only had two classrooms. The Headmaster lived in one of the cottages behind the school building. The school closed in 1928. The building was used as a Red Cross Centre from 1945 until 1967 and later as extra classrooms for the nearby Church of England School. Nurse Powell ran popular First Aid Classes there. Many years later the building became the village fish and chip shop.

Figure 81 – Children at The National School in 1898

The Church of England School

A Church of England all-age school was built near the Victorian School in 1928.

Figure 82 – The Church of England School (rear view)

The Lord Bishop of Gloucester came to Quedgeley on 30 April 1929 and a service of Dedication took place.

DEDICATION

OF THE

Church School Building

AT QUEDGELEY,

BY THE

LORD BISHOP OF GLOUCESTER,

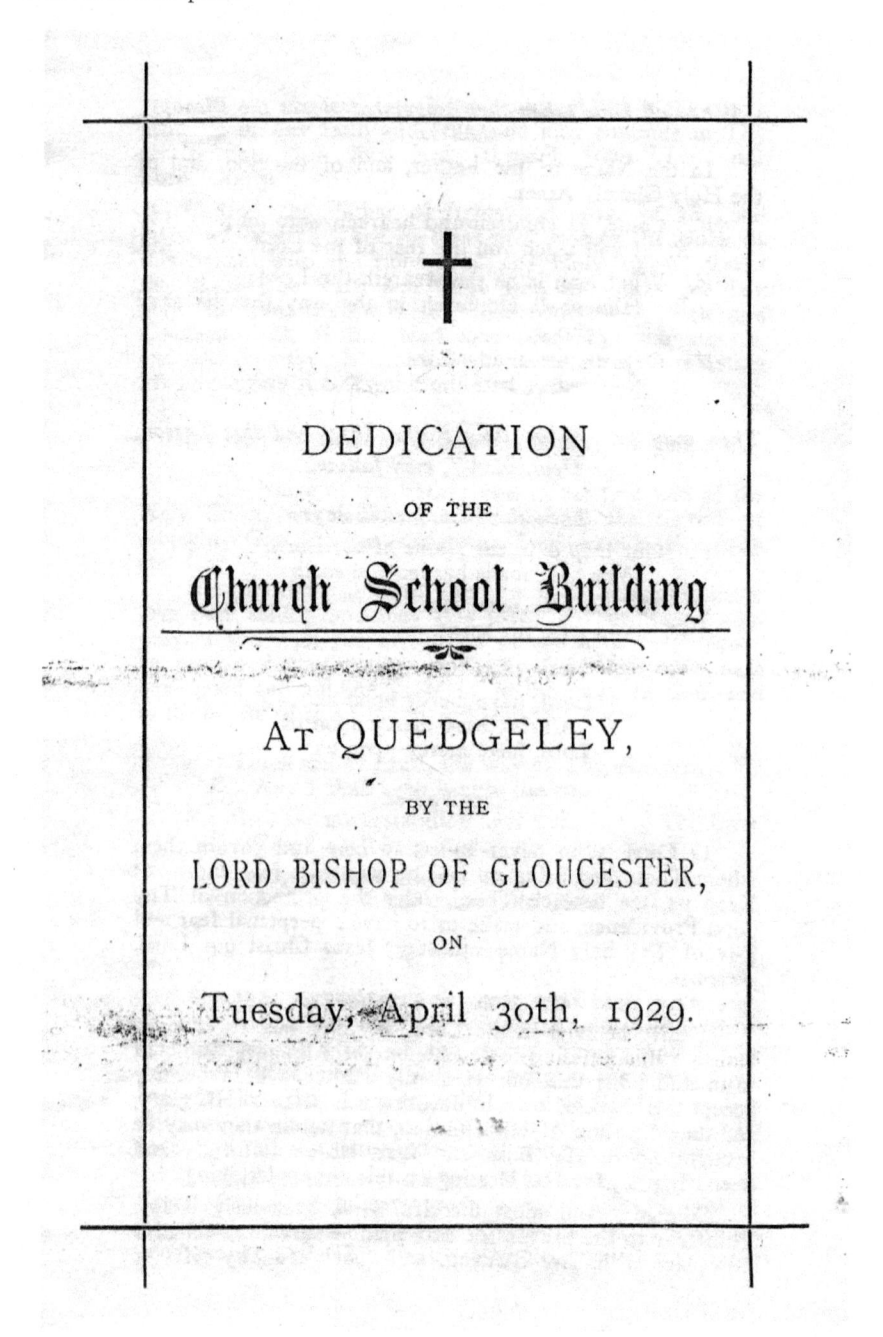

ON

Tuesday, April 30th, 1929.

Figure 83 – The Dedication Service of the Church of England School

Figure 84 – Children (Group 3) at The Church of England School (circa 1930)

The school had a very good reputation and continued right through the war years until 1951. The school then changed. The local infants and juniors were separated from the eleven-plus children. The school took in approximately 200 boys and girls aged over 11 from 12 surrounding village schools and doubled in size. The upper section became the new Quedgeley Secondary Modern School. Concrete buildings went up on the site to accommodate the influx which took some time to sort out.

Fred Winters, the Headmaster in 1952, at his first enlarged Speech Day in the Village Hall nearby, thanked the head boy Roy Townsend and head girl Valerie Cox for all their help. Figure 85 (on page 86) was taken in the Victorian School at Harvest Festival time. The front row (left to right) contains Margaret Shepherd (behind the flowers), Rosemary and Elizabeth Nash, Susan Parker, Jacqueline Hall, Jennifer Ely, Terry Bourne and Ann Turner. Behind them the adults are (left to right): Joan Bussey, Mona Robertson, a visiting Missionary and Fred Winters.

The school continued working in two separate sections until 1961 when the eleven-plus children moved out. In 1967 only 160 infants and juniors remained at the school. When the school eventually closed, the St James Centre was formed in the disused buildings.

Figure 85 – Children at the Church of England School in 1953

Severn Vale County Secondary Modern School

The new school opened lower down School Lane in 1961 and the fortunate eleven-plus children had spacious classrooms and wonderful facilities. By 1967 the school had 290 pupils. Many will remember Tony Lutkins who was Headmaster for 34 years from 1961 to 1995. He was supported by Gordon Blake, who first taught at the Quedgeley C. of E. School from 1957 and then moved with the pupils to Severn Vale in 1961. Gordon Blake finally retired in 1988, after over 30 years of service in Quedgeley.

Severn Vale had a big extension in 1982 offering 120 places in four excellent Science Laboratories, a Language room and two Humanities classrooms. The old science accommodation had been remodelled to provide first rate art and pottery facilities, complete with kiln room, print room and dark room. The following year the school had another extension to provide a gymnasium and new facilities for music, craft and geography. In 1987 Severn Vale became a Comprehensive School.

It was not always work and no play. Six adults took 42 pupils on a Mediterranean Cruise in 1990. They flew from Gatwick to Athens, where they boarded the luxury cruiser Odysseus. They visited Rhodes, Egypt, Israel and Turkey. The school had a £1,000,000 Sports Hall added in 1995. Leonard Spiers took over as Headmaster that year and looked after nearly 900 pupils. The school continues to thrive under the current headship.

Field Court Schools

By 1979 two new schools had been opened to accommodate the pupils from the Church of England School when it closed. They were the Field Court Voluntary-Controlled Infant School and the Field Court Junior School. They were built close to each other in Courtfield Road. Many will remember the teachers, Anne Mortimore, Mrs Chislett and David Stokes along with many more.

The schools ran completely independently but fostered close links, for the benefit of the children's educational continuity. By September 1984, many young children had arrived in Quedgeley and the Infant School was enlarged. The Junior School had the same problem and a new school was built on the Infant School's site. The large playing field was well-used. The Parent Teacher Association raised large sums of money to provide the children with extra books, equipment and parties.

After a team of five OFSTED Inspectors carried out a five-day inspection at Field Court Infant School, the only criticism levelled at the school was that some teachers worked too hard.

In 1993 the Junior School children planted trees for the 'Plant a tree for 93' initiative. Trees had been specially selected by conservation experts. Over 250 Junior School children also made a ceramic mural for the outside wall of the new library. I had an invitation to watch Gloucester's Town Crier, Alan Myatt, unveil the mural in September 1993.

Chapter 5 – Our Organisations and Clubs

Quedgeley Mothers' Union

In the past the members met at Quedgeley House and were hosted by the Curtis-Hayward Family. There were meetings before World War I, but I do not have any records. My mother joined them in the late 1930s and was a member for many years.

Today the Mothers' Union is the largest International Christian Organisation, with over 4 million members in 83 countries across the world having been founded by Mary Sumner in 1876.

When Quedgeley House Estate was sold in 1939, the Quedgeley members were welcomed by the Rector, Revd H Hadow at St James' Church Rectory. As a small child, I remember being collected from the infant school opposite The Rectory and sitting in the large cold dining room, while the members chatted and had tea.

Members arranged bazaars, coffee mornings and rummage sales in the Village Hall to support overseas missions and local charities. They also had very interesting speakers and film shows. The members took it in turn to clean the church brass and provide the church with flowers each week. I joined the Mothers' Union after I was married and soon became Secretary.

Years later in 1962 the Revd P Dack arrived with his mother and meetings carried on, with Mrs Dack as the enrolling member. Much work had been carried out in The Rectory and the meetings went well.

Unfortunately, when Revd Dack and his Mother left, the Mother's Union ended.

Figure 86 – Mothers' Union Annual Festival at the Cathedral in 1975

Gloucestershire Federation of Women's Institute

The Women's Institute was started in Stoney Creek, Ontario, Canada in 1897 and I visited the home where it started when they were celebrating their centenary in 1997.

Quedgeley Women's Institute started in 1925. Today there are now 140 active branches and just short of 5,000 members in Gloucestershire. All members belong to the National Federation of Women's Institutes. They are the largest women's organisation in the UK and they are also members of Associated Country Women of the World with branches in 70 countries.

The Women's Institute movement focuses on the education of women and their well-being, truth, tolerance and justice. The meetings are non-political and non-sectarian.

In 1925 meetings were held once a month in The Plough Hotel (Page 15). At the time Quedgeley was just a small country parish, with no street lighting, no electricity, mains water, or sewage systems to the houses.

When the Village Hall was built in 1928, by the side of the Bristol Road, the meetings were held there. Members always met on the second Wednesday of the month. With the loss of the Village Hall in 1958, plans had to be made for organisations and clubs to meet elsewhere. The Scout's Headquarters and The Red Cross Centre in School Lane nearby came in very handy. The new hall was opened in 1962 and the Quedgeley Women's Institute have been meeting there ever since.

Figure 87 – Quedgeley W.I. Meeting during a power cut in 1970

Chapter 5 – Our Organisations and Clubs   Page 91

Over the years the members have enjoyed interesting talks, film shows, carol concerts, coach trips, parties and trips to Cheltenham Theatre. Various classes have been taught in the hall including the keep fit class in Figure 88 showing (using their present names) Yvonne Harding (far left), Rosie Selby, Daphne Hogarth and Patricia Watts on the front row.

Figure 88 – Quedgeley W.I. Keep Fit Session in 1983

The Women's Institute's Denman College at Marcham, Oxon, was always a popular place to go to for a few days, but sadly it closed in 2020 and has now been sold.

The members enjoyed entering the Quedgeley Trust's Annual Show in the Village Hall and later at Severn Vale School (see Figure 89). It was a competition to see who could bake the best cake, make the best pickles, take the best photo and grow the biggest vegetables. It was sad when the Annual Show folded in the 2000s.

Figure 89 – Quedgeley W.I. win a prize in the Annual Show in 2005

Members have entered a team in The Quedgeley Annual Community Trust Quiz for many years and have done well. They also play skittles with other Women's Institutes on local alleys.

At the Annual General Meeting in November each year, a President, Secretary, Treasurer and Committee are selected for the following year. Like many other organisations, it is getting difficult to find people with the time to spare to fill these positions and some of the branches have now closed. I joined in 1952 and I am still a member in 2023.

Women's Institute Presidents from 1947

Mrs R. Chamberlayne: 1947-1950, 1954-1957, 1960 & 1961.

Mrs F. A. Winter: 1951-1953, 1958 & 1959.

Mrs S. Phipps: 1962-1964, 1987-1990.

Mrs D. McLaughlin: 1965-67, 1970-1972.

Mrs Radcliff: 1968 & 1969.

Mrs Screen: 1973-1975.

Mrs J. Leach: 1980.

Mrs J. Ryland: 1976-79, 1981 & 1982, 1991-1994, 1998- 2002.

Mrs M. Peacey: 1983-1986.

Mrs J. Freemantle: 1995-1997.

Mrs C. Meek: 2002-2004.

Mrs P. Watts: 2005-2023.

Quedgeley & District Youth Club

In the 1950s many teenagers joined the Youth Club and came to the original Village Hall once a week, to meet up with friends. They came on the bus, on their bikes, or walked. They organised games, talks and regular dances. Mrs Hooper and Mrs Boulter (sisters-in-law) brought the refreshments each week and everybody had a good time, including me. The club went well for years until we lost the Village Hall and the Youth Club had to close.

Once the new Village Hall was built and opened in 1962, the Quedgeley and District Youth Club could meet again. By 1964 the members were having physical education evening classes at Severn Vale School. At the Annual General Meeting in 1966, Peter

Phelps was Chairman, Ken Meek was Vice Chairman, William McLaughlin was Treasurer, Sylvia Phelps was Secretary and Leslie Ryland was the Club Leader. At that time the Club had 80 members on the books, with an average attendance of 65. Popular road walks were held in 1966, 1967, 1968 and 1969. The walks started from the Village Hall and went down the Bristol Road and turned into Elmore Lane, passed through Elmore, Longney, Hardwicke and back to Quedgeley, finishing with refreshments at The Retreat on Bristol Road. On average, 10 to 13 teams from all over Gloucestershire took part, with four club members in a team. The winning teams, who clocked up the shortest time on the walk, went away with Silver Cups.

In 1967 Sylvia and Peter Phelps left the district to run a post office. Ken Meek took over at the 1968 AGM. William Parsons became Vice Chairman, William Mc Laughlin carried on as Treasurer, Patricia Harding became Secretary and Mr Burrows took on the task of being Club Leader.

The club continued, enjoying camping holidays in the Forest of Dean, table tennis matches against other clubs, discos, billiards, darts and large fundraising fêtes in the Recreation Ground and at Severn Vale School. Mr J Maddox later became the Youth Club Leader.

Figure 90 – The RAF Commanding Officer opening a Youth Club Fête

Figure 91 – One of the Youth Club fêtes

By 1971 the membership at the club had dropped and a decision was taken at the AGM to close the club. The Adult Management Committee would not close the bank account, hoping things would improve. A year later another meeting was called. This time not enough adults came forward to form an Adult Management Committee. Time went on without a club and in 1979 Quedgeley Village Trust (formed in 1953 for the Queen's Coronation celebrations) called for interested people to come to a meeting in the Village Hall to discuss restarting the Youth Club. The County Youth and Community Officer would be attending to give advice. It was not until 1984, at a meeting in Gloucester, that the County Youth Officer of the day was asked to investigate leasing disused infant school buildings in School Lane, Quedgeley, for the local Youth Club. The buildings had other clubs running there. This old school site was now called the St James Centre. The Youth Club eventually moved in. Their Adult Management Committee received all the money from the 1970s folded club and used it to buy new equipment. At that time plans were also going ahead for a much-needed Community and Youth Centre. Finally, with the new centre plans agreed, building started in September 1994 and the new centre was opened in August 1995. The St James Centre was demolished and the Youth Club moved into their brand-new home and went from strength to strength.

Quedgeley Scouts, Cubs, Brownies and Rainbows

The Quedgeley Scouts started around 1952 and they met in the small brick building in The Rectory garden. Mr Cottrell, a postman living in Sims Lane, was the leader. In 1953 a Cub Pack was formed and they shared the same building. Later, Johnny Spence arrived to help with the Scouts and became the Leader, and Guy Selwyn looked after the Cubs. The Village Hall was later used for meetings. By 1957 the Troop soon realised they needed their own building. St James' Church had land available at the top of School Lane. When North Leach Prison advertised some of their wooden huts, Quedgeley Scouts went over to look at them. A wooden hut was purchased, but it had to be taken apart and moved to Quedgeley. Luckily, Johnny Spence was a greengrocer in Gloucester and had his own lorry. Help came forward and the hut was dismantled and transported safely on the lorry to School Lane.

Edgar Smith from Hardwicke was the Chairman of the Adult Management Committee for many years, John Clapton was Treasurer and Nancy Stroud was Secretary. Ivor Davis will be remembered for his time leading the Scouts, together with the help of his father, Dick. Philip Parker was also a popular Leader. In 1958, Philip took his family and a party of scouts to Luxembourg, which was a great success.

Figure 92 – Scout Trip to Luxembourg in 1958

Finally, on 29 November 1959 the Scouts moved into their new Headquarters. We were so grateful to the Scout and Cub movement in Quedgeley for the care and education it gave to the local children. They were well-trained to get their special badges. They enjoyed outings, walks, camps and BBQs. Our own sons, Adrian and Nicholas, enjoyed many happy years in the Cubs, then the Scouts. Mrs Warrener and her daughter ran the Cubs for a long time.

Figure 93 – Cub Pack with Cub Leader Mrs Warrener

Once a year the Scouts would tour the village and knock on the doors during 'Bob a Job Week', which could involve washing a car or doing a bit of weeding. Special Scouts and Cub Services were held at St James' Church nearby and the Troop would proudly march down School Lane to the Church, carrying their banners looking very smart. Often the group had a waiting list to join.

Years later, Hardwicke Girl Guides moved to the Quedgeley Scout's Headquarters, when they could not use Hardwicke Old School, and it worked out well. Later, Elmore started a Girl Guide Group and the Guides went there. Pat Evans looked after the Quedgeley Beavers, who were too young to be in the Cubs. Also, the local Brownies and Rainbows met on another night. By 1988 there were 250 youngsters using the hut during the week. It was decided that the hut needed an overhaul. It had been running for nearly 30 years and had never been officially opened. Weeks of painting and repairs took place. Her Royal Highness Princess Margaret Rose, as President of the Girl Guides, was asked to come to open the Headquarters, which she accepted on 22 June 1988. We waited in School Lane to see her arrive in the large chauffeur- driven car, together with the Lord-Lieutenant of Gloucestershire.

Figure 94 – The late Princess Margaret visiting The Rainbows

Infant Welfare Clinic

It was one of the longest-running activities ever to keep going in Quedgeley. The first group of mothers and babies met in 1916 at Quedgeley House, on the estate belonging to the Curtis-Hayward family, near St James' Church.

From 1928 the group moved into the newly-built Village Hall. My mother, Sybil Ely, took a very active part in the running of the Welfare Clinic from the late 1930s and in time was elected President, a position she held for many years. The small babies, including my sister and I, had to be undressed and weighed.

In 1958 after the Village Hall was destroyed, the clinic had to move to the Methodist Chapel on Bristol Road and The Red Cross Centre on School Lane. The new Village Hall was opened in 1962 and the clinic moved back for many years.

Mothers had transport laid on to collect them from the surrounding villages. The grateful mums would talk to the visiting Health Visitors with their problems or wait to see the doctor in her room. They would collect the baby's tins of dried milk and bottles of orange juice and finish up with tea provided by the wonderful Granny Veale who had helped with the welfare since it was founded. She lived to a great age and shared her Parklands flat with her daughter, Joan Veale, and her other daughter, Betty Page, and family also lived near her.

When my mother retired from the Committee, I carried on as President. We had fundraising events to provide the mothers and babies with a Christmas party and buy the babies a present.

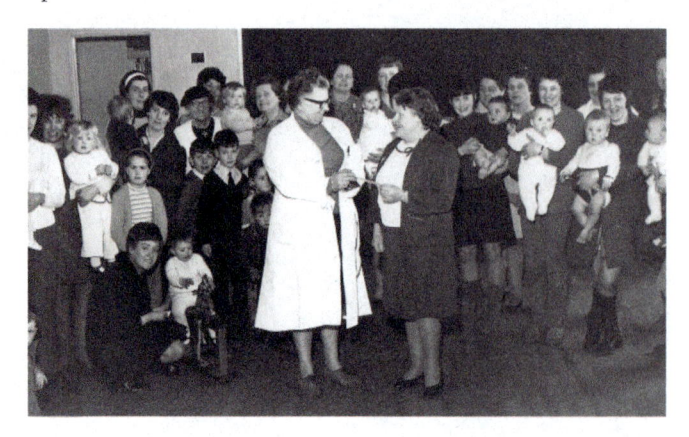

Figure 95 – Infant Welfare's Nurse Carpenter with Margaret Uzzell in 1965

Nancy Stroud had been a loyal, hard-working Committee Member for 26 years and took on the position of President from me. In 1990 the new Quedgeley Health Campus was opened 100 yards from the Village Hall, behind Tesco. The Quedgeley & District Welfare Clinic ceased by name and the NHS took over the management. The clinic continued with the help of volunteers until late 1994.

The Severn NHS Trust invited all the past Welfare Committee's to the Quedgeley Well Baby Clinic for a reunion, held on Tuesday 14 March 1995, 3:00pm, at Quedgeley Clinic *"To mark the end of a very happy era and to say farewell and thank you to the volunteers who so kindly put aside their time to help for many years until Christmas 1994"*. We were all pleased to receive a carriage clock. It was the end of a very happy era. In Figure 96 we can see (left to right): Mrs C Meek, Mrs N Stroud, Mrs J Ryland, Mrs J Hart, Mrs V Overthrow, Mrs B Page, Mrs S Ely and standing at the back, Mrs Y Harding.

Figure 96 – Infant Welfare Committee Goodbye Presentation

Quedgeley Golden Age

Mrs Cook started the idea of forming a club for the over 60s. Quedgeley Village Hall was the ideal place to hold a club. A meeting was arranged and, by 8 July 1968, the club was up and running. At the first meeting, 12 pensioners met and by Christmas there were 85 sitting down to the Christmas lunch. The club received a loan from the Women's Royal Voluntary Service and the name 'Golden Age' was chosen. Wilfred Brunt, a retired farmer from Brookthorpe, was one of the earliest elected Chairman and Kathleen Screen from Hardwicke, the Secretary. Lady Guise from Elmore Court was asked to be President, which she accepted. The club would meet on the first and third Tuesday of the month from 2:00pm to 4:00pm. This was the start of many years of happy social gatherings.

Over the years the club had outstanding leaders like Ursula Norman (known as Sue), who was also the Warden to the Pensioners at nearby St James Close. Quizzes, bingo afternoons, talks, films, entertainers, days out to Weston-Super-Mare, trips to the theatre at Cheltenham, shopping trips to Worcester, coach holidays by the sea, were well supported and of course Christmas Dinners in the Village Hall.

In the 1990s the members were busy taking part in a marathon knitting exercise for charity. Mary Hinder and Mary Newcombe, both 93 years old, joined 23 other club members in knitting 36 blankets for the Women's Royal Voluntary Service. It was three months' work and members either knitted or crocheted woollen squares, or whole blankets (see Figure 97). The Women's Royal Voluntary Service then distributed the blankets to their own home care service for the elderly, Manor Day Home in Barnwood and Gloucestershire Royal Hospital's maternity ward.

Figure 97 – The Golden Age Club knitters in 1993

In 1993 glasses were raised and a toast was made to Quedgeley's Golden Age Club on reaching its twenty-fifth year. The Leader, Mrs Norman, gave a brief history of the club and welcomed Beryl Penfold, daughter of Mrs Cook who started the club. Many original members were there, including Mrs Bailey, Mrs Marsh, Mrs Huggins, Mrs Ely, Mrs K Screen and Mrs E Smith who had both made tea for the club for the whole 25 years.

The Club sadly folded in 2022 after running for 54 years, mainly due to the COVID-19 outbreak.

Quedgeley Town Council

Years ago I had the following handed to me by Mr Graham G Stroud JP which I kept and found to be interesting. I hope you think so too.

What are Parish/Town Councils?

Parish Councils are the lowest tier of Local Government Administration, coming under the current higher levels of District and County Councils. They came into existence under the Local Government Act of 1894 and only apply to Rural Areas, although it is now permissible to have comparable Ward Councils in towns.

Some smaller parishes have never had Parish Councils and only operate on an Annual Parish Meeting. Villages with Parish Councils must also have an Annual Parish Meeting usually held in March. At these meetings the Parish Council Chairman presides and presents to the Parishioners a resume of the previous year's work of the Parish Council. Parish Representatives on various bodies, report on their work. Members of the public may raise matters concerning the Parish and pass Resolutions thereon. The Parish Meeting is only advisory and the Parish Council are not bound by any resolution. Parish meetings may be called at other times, as decided by the Parish Council on matters of specific interest in the Village. Issues are decided by a show of hands unless a poll is demanded by ten or more Electors.

Parish Councillors are elected by secret ballot and usually serve for three years, all retiring at the same time. At the first meeting of the Parish Council after the Election, which must be held within fourteen days of the declaration of the Poll, Councillors must sign the Acceptance Book of Office, before business commences. Any absentees must sign before the commencement of business at the next meeting.

First Quedgeley Parish Council

The first election to the Quedgeley Parish Council was carried out at a Parish Meeting held in the Dame School on 4 December 1894. There is no record of how many Parishioners attended, but seven nominations were made for five seats, resulting in the following candidates being elected.

RALPH BROWNING – FARMER, EDWARD BRYANS - CLERK IN HOLY ORDERS, SYDNEY LANE – MERCHANT, JAMES NEWCOMBE – LABOURER, JAMES RYDER - GARDENER

Chapter 5 – Our Organisations and Clubs

At their first meeting on 19 December 1894, they elected Lieutenant Colonel Curtis-Hayward to be Chairman, although he had not been a candidate for Office. Mr R Browning became Vice Chairman. The Assistant Overseer of the Poor for the Parish, Mr Hooper, became Clerk. Mr George Pike, Manager of the Capital and Counties Bank was appointed Treasurer, although it was not clear from the Minutes as to whether this was to the Overseer or the Parish Council. It would seem to be the former, as there is a minute record that the demand be made on the Overseer, for a sum to defray the expenses of the Parish Council. Unfortunately, the early financial records are not available but it would appear that the Clerk's salary was £2 per annum. It is doubtful whether these earlier proceedings were legal, as no signatures of Acceptance of Office were made. Difficulties of obtaining a good attendance at the Annual Parish Meeting were evident, as early as the first such meeting held on 16 April 1895. Lieutenant Colonel Curtis-Hayward took the Chair but found one Parish Councillor, Revd E Bryans to support him. Three members of the public namely Mr S Cale, Mr F Knight and Mr W Hooper. The Minute book records curtly "No business was transacted and the meeting adjourned". The current Councillors apparently continued in Office, as no further elections are recorded in the Minute Book until the Annual Parish Meeting on 9 March 1896. Mr Ralph Browning, Mr James Ryder and Mr James Newcombe, who by now had worked his way up from Labourer to Journeyman Baker, were all elected. They were joined by Mr Henry Merrett (farmer) and Mr William Robinson (gentleman). For some reason unstated, the nomination of Cllr. Sydney Lane was declared invalid.

At the Parish Council Meeting on 16 April 1896 a committee was established to investigate the need for a public water supply. It duly reported in June 1896. Mr Boyce was willing to give a portion of his garden for the siting of a parish pump, near where the Howborn Green brook crosses the Bristol Road. Estimated cost of digging a well twelve feet deep and six feet in diameter together with a pump was £25. Ratepayers did not like to spend money, if they could avoid doing so and on being put to a Parish Meeting in July 1896 the scheme was rejected, only one vote being recorded in favour.

October 1897 reported the receipt of two letters from the Town Clerk of the City of Gloucester regarding the proposed extension of the City Boundary. The Parish Council offered no opposition and did not think a Parish Meeting desirable. A somewhat different attitude to that expected today.

In April 1898 the earliest recorded difficulty at Naas Lane Railway Crossing appears, when it was reported the Company were in the habit of locking the gate at Naas crossing, during a portion of the day on Sundays and were consequently reported to the District Council.

The Minutes become somewhat more legible from April 1900, due to the local Schoolmaster, T Beacall taking over the post of Clerk, combining it with Assistant Overseer of the Poor, at a combined salary of £16 per annum. He was however obviously new to the job and omitted to ensure the Councillors signed the Acceptance of Office Book, resulting in the Council having to petition the County Council, who on 4 May 1901 issued a County of Gloucester (Removal of Difficulties No2) Order 1901 allowing the Councillors to sign on 10 June 1901 and to have effect, as if they had been signed on the original date.

Rates were to the fore in April 1904 when an increase of the Precept was requested by the Gloucester

Union. It was thought to be excessive and the Clerk was instructed to write and ask for it to be reduced.

There were still difficulties with Annual Parish Meetings. Minutes show that the notice of the Annual Meeting was published for 29 March 1906. The Clerk attended the Schoolroom, but no members of the public attended. Presumably the existing Councillors soldiered on, as there is no evidence of another election till the Parish Meeting in 1907. Procedure still left a lot to be desired in as much as the Chairman being ill, the Clerk T Beacall took the Chair.

At the Parish Meeting on 14 March 1910, we get the first recorded details of the voting for Parish Councillors: six candidates, five were successful all receiving seven votes with the runner up getting four votes.

The first Special Parish Meeting took place on 1 May 1911 to make arrangements to celebrate the Coronation of King George V and Queen Mary. Festivities to take place on Saturday, 8 July 1911. Tea and presentation of Coronation Mugs to children. Meat tea for adults, dancing on the lawn at Quedgeley House and sports in the park by permission of Mr L Carter. A tent to be erected.

Allotments were being requested by September 1911, but on being advised of a suggested rent of £4 per acre per annum, the fifteen applicants declined to pursue the matter.

Only the Chairman and Clerk attended the Annual Parish Meeting in 1911 and 1912, so no elections took place between 1910 and 1913. On 17 March 1913 there were five nominations for five seats, so no need for a vote. Those elected were Mr J Vick (Waterwells Farm), Mr C Oliver (Yew Tree Villas), Mr James Pitt (Field Court Farm), Mr Henry Lovell (Highcliffe Farm) and Revd F Grenside (The Rectory) with Lieutenant Colonel Curtis-Hayward as the Chairman. Parish meetings went back to normal 1914/1915. No attendances by the parishioners in 1916/17/18. In 1919 we did have attendance, J Vick, C Oliver and J Pitts being re-elected and Revd Bartlett replaced Revd F Grenside who had left the Parish and Josiah C White of The Villa, replaced F Lovell. Back to square one in 1920. Mrs E Fisher became Clerk in April 1921 when T Beacall retired but she had resigned by September and was replaced by Mr C Oliver who had an unfortunate death in June 1922 (he took his own life in the Gloucester & Sharpness Canal). He was followed by Mr George and in 1923 by Arthur Witchell. Lieutenant Colonel Curtis-Hayward died in 1924. He was Chairman for thirty years. Reginald Curtis-Hayward became the next Chairman of the Parish Council.

In March 1924, plans for a Village Hall were being considered, cost of estimates varying from £900 to £1,000. Fund raising activities took place. £450 being handed in by March 1926. There the matter disappears. In January 1928 the new Village Hall was built and opened. The Parish Council elected Mr R Curtis-Hayward to serve on the committee.

By April 1929 the technological revolution overtook us. It was complained that the petrol pump operated near the Plough Inn by Mr W Allen was a danger to the public. The supply arm being too *long, forcing pedestrians to walk in the roadway liable to be involved in a traffic accident and it needed urgent attention. No reply by Mr Allen by September 1929 and the matter was dropped.*

On 1 January 1932, the recreation field on Bristol Road, transferred from Mr Reginald Curtis-Hayward, who held it in trust on behalf of the Parish, to the Parish Council. This was obviously the outcome of years of wrangling about the monies received from any rent of the field which had never been paid to the Parish Council but had been used for Church School expenditure. Attempts to recover these monies for the Parish Council were unsuccessful and then the matter was dropped. It is interesting to note however, in April 1932, Mr J C White JP became Chairman in place of Mr R Curtis-Hayward.

September 1932 Mr H Mansfield became Clerk to the Parish Council, continuing in Office till his death in 1956, when he was followed by his son Kenneth.

In March 1935, two additional Parish Councillors were authorised bringing the number up to seven. Mr E Vaile had sixteen votes and Mr E J Boulter fifteen votes being elected.

On 6 May 1935, King George V and Queen Mary celebrated their Jubilee year. There was a Church service in the morning, pensioners lunch, procession to the field, followed by sports, children's tea party and a dance for adults, in the evening.

The Rural District Council in Gloucester were considering laying a water main through Quedgeley and other Parishes south of Gloucester at a cost of a 6d rate for the Parishes concerned. Quedgeley considered it was not satisfactory unless side roads were also served.

In 1936, the question of house refuse collection was raised. As the cost would equate to a 3d rate, it was agreed not to participate.

A house-to-house collection for the King George V Memorial Fund raised £5-7-10d. Quedgeley was the first parish in the county to forward their contribution.

In 1937, council housing was discussed at the parish meeting. The site was to be Sims Lane. One pair was considered sufficient.

In October 1938, Mr A E Morgan representing the Parish Council at a conference, had opposed the Election of Parish Councillors by Poll.

On 7 November 1939, Mr E Boulter raised the question of gifts to local men serving with HM Forces and undertook fund raising activities, thus enabling twenty persons to receive 120 cigarettes and a money order at Christmas 1939.

In July 1940, the construction of public air raid shelters was under discussion but found to be too costly. The Parish Council however undertook to construct trenches in the recreation field. These to be safe and properly drained. Mr E Boulter undertook the work at an estimated £15. He did not proceed due to difficulties and rescinded in February 1941.

Scrap iron was also to be collected for the war effort. Mrs L Prout of Severn Farm, offering to collect this with her car and trailer and bring it to the site, offered by Hawkes Bakery, Bristol Road.

Wings for Victory Week 8 to 15 May 1941. Big sale of bonds, certificates, mock auction etc, realised the magnificent sum of £6,935. Not bad for a small village.

July 1941 saw the village communications improved, with the erection of a telephone kiosk outside the recreation field. In September 1941, the Defence Committee was established, consisting of the Parish Council and ten other members, representing various organisations and six juveniles as messengers. The Committee thereafter acted independently of the Parish Council. In March 1942, the Parish meeting elected twenty parishioners to form the Village Hall committee.

The County Planning Officer, in October 1942 undertook a survey of parish amenities. The Parish Council requested sewage, road lighting, more shops, bus shelters and a public convenience.

By April 1943 there was trouble with the ditch at the bottom of the recreation field silting up and on inspection was found to be due to action of a Mr Lee banking up the ditch where it ran through the adjoining parish allotments, to obtain water for his ducks. He had not removed the obstruction as requested by June and was given seven days to comply, otherwise it would be removed for him.

In October 1944, the Welcome Home Fund was established for returning members of HM Forces at the end of the hostilities. Christmas gifts to village members of the Forces which had operated from 1939 were to continue. On closure in October 1946 £559 had been raised.

In November 1945, the Gloucester Corporation Bill to extend the City Boundary was considered. The Parish Council raised the strongest possible objections. This view was endorsed at a Parish Council Meeting.

In April 1945, the old Victorian Dame School was to be developed as a Welfare Centre. There was also a request made to the Rural District Council, for a hundred houses to be erected in the Village. It took till 1952 before Parklands site of sixteen houses came to fruition. The twenty-six flats were added in 1955.

In March 1946, Cllr. E J Boulter reported on the Rural District Council meeting, where advice had been received. Gloucester Corporation were to proceed with a compulsory purchase order for 400 acres in the village. The Parish Council strongly condemned the action and agreed to oppose it.

A poll took place in 1946 for Parish Councillors at the Annual Meeting. Mr A J Boulter, Mr R S Williams, Mr E Vaile, Mr R S Worrall, Mr C Morse, Mr L Carter and Mr F A Winter, the School Master were elected.

In January 1947, accidents on the main road were causing concern and it was agreed to apply for a speed limit of thirty miles per hour through the village.

In June 1951, the Midlands Electricity Board promised street lighting by the autumn, for the Bristol

Road from School Lane to the Hardwicke boundary. Street lighting for Sims, Elmore, School and Naas Lanes was installed in 1959 at a cost of £161.

In 1960, proposals from Glevum Estates, who had purchased Woolstrop Farm, were received to build a new town of 1,500 houses thereon. The development to include two new schools, two churches, a swimming pool with new main road connecting to the roundabout at the city boundary. Part of the plan happened twenty years later.

Bungalows for pensioners were built in St James Close, School Lane in 1961 and more added later, together with resident warden accommodation and a communal room.

The end of Quedgeley Parish Council extracts.

If you wish to find out more, visit the Gloucester Archives Office in Alvin Street, Gloucester, where you can find the following Quedgeley Minute Books:

Book 1: 1894 to 1936, 42 years; **Book 2**: 1937 to 1952, 15 years;

Book 3: 1953 to 1960, 7 years; **Book 4**: 1961 to 1964, 3 years and more.

Recent Quedgeley Parish Council

For many years, Quedgeley was in the Gloucester Rural District Council area and had elections every three years. That all changed in 1973 when six new Districts were formed: Gloucester, Cheltenham, Cotswolds, Forest of Dean, Tewkesbury and Stroud. Quedgeley was placed in the new Stroud District Council.

The candidates standing lived in the village most of their lives. The Council had people of all ages and they always stood as Independents. They were farmers, teachers, shopkeepers, local tradesmen and professional women. They all served for many years, giving their very best.

In 1986 Chairman Ken Meek asked for the number of Parish Councillors to be increased, due to the heavy workload. This was duly granted, increasing from 12 to 17 councillors, and this would start from the forthcoming Parish Election on 7 May 1987.

At the Chairman's final monthly Parish Council meeting in April 1987, he paid tribute to William Parsons (known as Jack) who had recently died. Jack had been a hardworking faithful councillor for seventeen years and would be greatly missed. The Clerk, Jean Field, was leaving the council after ten years of excellent service. The Revd and Mrs Field were both retiring and moving to Wales. The Parish Council was also losing four very experienced councillors who were retiring after clocking up 44 years of service between them: Jon Boulter, Ronald Jowett, Cyril Mayo and Philip

Parker.

The 7 May 1987 Parish Council Election day was one to remember. For the first time, politics played a big part. The Liberal Alliance Party canvassed the villages of Quedgeley and Hardwicke. They wanted the "*old guard out*".

On polling day, Quedgeley parishioners had a two-feet long ballot paper with 34 names on it. They had to select 17 names. The queue was so long, many didn't vote. In both parishes, most of the existing councillors lost their seats.

The new Quedgeley Parish Councillors frequently found that they could not agree and their meetings often went on until midnight. Some resigned and did not complete their first term of office. The Clerk constantly advertised for replacements.

From 1st April 1991 Quedgeley moved from Stroud District Council into Gloucester City Council and paid council taxes for all the services. Quedgeley became one of the City's 12 Wards. It was the only ward paying an extra council tax to provide a Parish Council.

After many years a poll was held in 2005, to find out whether or not, the residents of Quedgeley wanted a Parish Council. This was arranged with only 5 hours of voting and no postal votes. It was a low turnout, with almost equal votes cast. The Gloucester City Council decided to let the Quedgeley Parish Council continue for another year. 12 years later in 2017, the Quedgeley Parish Council voted itself to become a Town Council.

Figure 98 – Parish Council Beating The Bounds in 1979

Chapter 5 – Our Organisations and Clubs

Figure 99 – The opening of the first Parish Council Office on 29 January 1993

The following years to 2000 we saw Quedgeley's green and pleasant land covered with new homes and businesses becoming a popular and convenient place to live and work.

Figure 100 – The expansion of new homes in Quedgeley

Quedgeley Community Trust

In 1977, the year of the late Queen Elizabeth's Silver Jubilee, Quedgeley Village Trust was formed by Mr Graham G Stroud (known as Tony). Tony was elected Chairman with Mrs Jean Turner as Secretary with a very good working Committee.

The residents in Quedgeley were very grateful for all the new events that the Committee had set up over the years. They organized the Silver Jubilee celebrations and monthly discos for the young in the Village Hall. They started the first Annual Village Produce Show which continued for years. The Quedgeley Village Trust helped form the Quedgeley Entertainers Group which produced wonderful shows each year. A firework display was held annually in the Recreation Ground and later at the RAF Headquarters.

In 1928 the Curtis-Hayward family transferred some land in School Lane into the hands of the Gloucester Diocesan Trust. A Church of England School was built there and was used for many years. In the 1990s, the Gloucester Diocesan Trust was abandoned and the land was given free of charge (but with many restrictions) to the Quedgeley Parish Council to build the Quedgeley Youth and Community Centre *"To promote the benefit of the inhabitants of Quedgeley, to advance education and provide facilities"*. The Gloucestershire County Council had an interest in the youth section of the Centre and provided funds towards the building.

The Quedgeley Community Trust was set up on 23 July 1997 to look after the large Youth and Community Centre. It was an unincorporated association and a registered Charity. The Quedgeley Community Trust was a much larger organisation and replaced the Quedgeley Village Trust. The Executive/General Committee Members at that time were: Mr K Tudor (Chairman), Miss M E Allison, Miss A C Balchin, Mr K & Mrs J Freemantle, Mr M Glanville, Mrs J Hanks, Mr T Hughes, Mr A M Jarrett, Mrs C J Meek, Mr K Miller, Mrs J Ryland, Mr J Standing and Mr G Trower. The Quedgeley Community Trust looked after the Youth and Community Centre for five years and then Quedgeley Parish Council took over the management.

Quedgeley News was the Quedgeley Community Trust's best source of income and hundreds of magazines were produced each month. The group met in the Village Hall and the magazine bundles were be given to 87 volunteers who delivered them around the village. The Trust created a limited company called Quedgeley News Ltd to undertake certain activities which were considered to constitute trade. The company was set up and four custodian trustees agreed to hold a share for the Quedgeley Community Trust. The profits were handed to the Trust who in turn helped many local organizations with thousands of pounds. The Quedgeley Rector Geoffrey Stickland, Keith Freemantle, John Standing, Caroline Meek, and Jacqueline Hall (who had replaced John Standing after his death) all stayed on as Share Holders, until Quedgeley News folded in December 2019.

Chapter 6 – Our People

The Curtis-Hayward Family

In the middle of the seventeenth century William Hayward of Forthampton near Tewkesbury, purchased Woolstrop Manor (later named Quedgeley House Estate). He died in 1696. His son, William, married Margaret, eldest daughter of General Selwyn of Matson. They had issue Thomas, John and Albinia; John entered the Church; Daughter Albinia married Thomas Winstone of Oldbury Court Gloucestershire; Thomas succeeded in the estates after his father's death in 1709.

His son, also called Thomas, took possession in 1732. He died in 1781. His son Charles then succeeded his father who was a bachelor; when he died in 1803 the estates went to his brother William. Now William also inherited (his uncle) Thomas Winstone's property, at Oldbury Court. William then added Winstone onto his Hayward surname. William and his wife had one son who died in 1797, and three daughters. The eldest of these, Albinia Francis Hayward who married the Revd John Adey Curtis, Rector of Bitton in 1799; Albinia then added Curtis onto her family name. Their eldest son, John Curtis-Hayward, was born in 1804. The Revd John Adey died in 1812. His widow Albinia succeeded to the Quedgeley House Estate after her father's death in 1818. Her family moved from Bath, into Quedgeley House.

Albinia died in 1860 and her son, John Curtis-Hayward, MA, JP married Elizabeth, daughter of Benjamin Harrison Esq. of Clapham Common. They had two sons and five daughters. John Curtis-Hayward MA, JP was thrown from his horse on his way back from a meeting in Gloucester and died shortly afterwards in May 1874. It then passed to his son Lieutenant Colonel John Frederick Curtis-Hayward JP who held many important positions in the County. He died in 1923.

The estate then passed to his nephew, Reginald Curtis-Hayward, which surprised John's brother, Miles, and other members of the family. Miles is mentioned in this book as a Trustee of the first Quedgeley Village Hall. Miles farmed in the south of Gloucester and together with his wife had three sons: John Curtis-Hayward, the Very Reverend Canon Tom Curtis-Hayward (1926 to 2001) and Miles Carlyon Curtis-Hayward (1929 to 2011).

Reginald Curtis-Hayward sold Quedgeley House to the Quedgeley Estate Company in 1939. This was the end of the Curtis-Hayward family connection with Quedgeley.

The Cale Family (1862 to date)

In 1927 there were three basket makers in the parish, all working near the Bristol Road. By the end of the twentieth century only Richard Cale was still in business. His grandfather, Frederick Cale, (1862 to 1949) had started the business and then his son, Jack Cale (1901 to 1979), continued his work, eventually passing it on to his son, Richard. They were all fine craftsmen and were kept very busy.

Figure 101 – Frederick Cale (1862-1949)

Chapter 6 – Our People   Page 111

Figure 102 – Jack Cale (1901-1979)

Figure 103 – Jack Cale (left) with son Richard Cale

Mary Beacall (1883 to 1966)

Mary Beacall died in 1966 at the age of 83 and during her last years jotted down some of her early recollections of Quedgeley. These were edited by the youngest member of the family, Phyllis, who died in 1992. It must have been in 1888 that Mary's father moved with his young and growing family from Peak Forest in Derbyshire to become the village Schoolmaster in Quedgeley. This is Mary's earliest recollection of their arrival.

I can recall with delight our first view of the lane where the schoolhouse stood. There were bright little celandines blooming on the grass verges and this was quite a new sight to Tom and me (aged seven and five respectively).

The first person to greet us was old Mrs Cook, the sexton's wife, whose cottage adjoined the schoolhouse. She was a dear old lady who looked so sweet and comely in her little mutch and shawl and full bunchy skirt. She used to keep bees, I remember, and when they swarmed, she would go out, swathed in a large hat and veil, and 'tang' them by banging on a tin tray with a shovel. She couldn't read, so whenever she had a letter from her grandson, she would bring it round for mother to read it to her.

She was always gentle in her speech, with never a coarse word. Once she told mother she had heard of a queen who was so bad that they called her 'Badword Mary'!

She accompanied her husband to all the services (on weekdays as well as Sundays) and joined in his long drawn-out " Ay-men". He was quite sure that the Rector couldn't have done without him, for, as he said, "I puts it all out ready for 'im, and 'e only 'as to read it out". He usually had a few 'bulls eyes' in his pocket and would share them with us children. They were sometimes rather fluffy from his pocket but, of course, we didn't mind that!

Quedgeley village straggled along the main road (from Gloucester to Bristol). There were half a dozen large farms, some with interesting names like Woolstrop, Dawes, Field Court and Highcliffe. There was also Queen Anne's Farm, with a beautiful, thatched roof. Here King Henry VIII and Anne Boleyn were reputed to have spent a night! A carrier's van passed through the village about three times a week, and passengers or parcels could be taken to Gloucester. Some of the original village green still remained, where villagers could pasture their cattle free of charge, and where cricket, somewhat homemade could be played. Apart from the carrier's van, people either walked or rode bicycles or tricycles, and even 'penny farthings' were sometimes seen. Later on came "Gardener's Bus" which plied to Gloucester from the "Morning Star" at Hardwicke three times a day - a great luxury! The other vehicles you would see would be farm carts or pony traps. We were always taken to Gloucester in the shoemaker's trap at the start of our annual holiday. The great moment was the pony's sudden spurt up the slope to G.W.R. station.

We always took our boots to be mended by this shoemaker, for he was a good craftsman and used excellent leather. "There's nothing like leather", he was fond of saying. His shop, which was in his own house, was not far from the "Plough" inn, the one public house in the village. There was one main shop the grocers, and a meat shop to which we went in the middle of the week when the Sunday joint was finished. I never liked going there as the smell of stale meat was not appetizing. But the owner was a man of some education, and a very desirous that other people might have the same chance. Our main joint of meat came from "Austy Brooks" of Hardwicke, who used to call for our orders and give information on the meat he could offer that week. For example, "Me legs is heavy", he would say!

In those early days there was no District Nurse, only one of the Sairey Gamp variety - a very kindly dame who stood for many of the babies at their christening and uttered loud responses in the wrong places.

The Rector's wife at that time, however, was an expert nurse, who midwifed many of the village women and helped them to rear their large families. She had a large family herself and must have been thrifty, for she was reputed to eke out their meals with puffballs and cold porridge!

Among the 'helps' who came to assist in the work of our own large family was Mrs Bailey, a notable washerwoman, with short curly hair, whose invariable remark when she arrived was, "Oh, I be that tired", but who bustled about and got a line of washing up in no time. For her mid-morning refreshment, she liked beer, heated by being stirred with a red-hot poker! A much later washerwoman was Miss Cowmeadow, affectionately called "Cowie" behind her back. Her scrubbing was as slow and thorough as her speech, in which most words of one syllable became two. "Go-ood ni-ight, Miss Cowmeadow", said my naughty young brother once, ""Go-ood ni-ight, Si-ir", she replied, unaware that he was laughing at her. Another remark of hers that I recall was her comment upon the pale grey suit that my sister had prepared for her honeymoon. "It'oull do nicely for 'alf mourning".

The church and the Rectory, as well as the school, stood in a lane off the main road, in the middle of the village. The church, which had originally been served by monks from Llanthony Abbey, was dedicated to St. James, whose scallop shell appeared on the banner. There was a fine peal of bells, rung to usher in Christmas and New Year, with a muffled peal on Holy Innocents' Day.

In my childhood, church played a big part in our lives. Every Sunday morning, after Sunday school (in the dayschool building) we galloped along the line to church for Matins. Evensong was not compulsory, and therefore more of a treat, especially as the candles were lighted; and festivals were even more exciting.

At Harvest Festival every available open space was filled with huge marrows, well-scrubbed potatoes and turnips, and well-polished apples. So many people came then that chairs had to be put in the aisles to seat them, and the choir processed from the south door to the altar, their leader carrying the banner.

Once arrived there he would turn round to face the congregation so that we could all see the banner with the name QUEDGELEY on it in large letters, which we thought the finest thing in the world. In order to enter by the south door the choir had to go outside from the vestry and make their way round between the tombstones! One of the Rectors told us that on one occasion his gravity was *sorely shaken by the sight of Rags, his dog, who had managed to get a jampot stuck over one ear!*

There were some good male voices in the choir. Father trained them to sing as if they enjoyed it, especially in the Magnificat, when they seemed really rejoicing, especially one farmer with a lovely rounded bass, who always turned to face the congregation as he sang, "and 'oly is 'is Name".

Some of these voices were also much in demand at village concerts, held in the school. One duet between two of them entitled "The Upper Ten and the Lower Five" was always greatly appreciated.

Sometimes, too, there would be trios, sung by mother (who had a good contralto voice) with the Rector's wife and one of the ladies from Quedgeley House. Besides these concerts in those early days there were sometimes "Penny Readings". But the best and most enjoyable entertainment happened at Christmas, with the visit of the wassailers, or "waysailors" as they pronounced it. How quickly we children jumped out of bed when we heard them coming and, hastily donning a few clothes, rushed downstairs to see them! They came dressed in smocks, and one main carried a small Christmas tree, decorated with balls and tinsel, and with a money box underneath. They would begin their singing with the greeting,

"Way-sa-wil, way-sa-il, to be jolly way-sa-il

And a jolly way-sa-il we drink unto thee."

They would then proceed with an old song about the old woman who "ad a pet cow, but 'ow to maintain 'er she did not know 'ow". This famous cow was named Colley, and the song continued with wishing good health to her and every part of her in turn, with appropriate good wishes to the audience. For example, there was "ealth unto Colley and to 'er right eye, and a-wishing yer masters a good New Year's pie". Later the toast was "to Colley and to 'er right leg, and a-wishing yer masters a good New Year's pig, and so on. When the whole of Colley was satisfactorily disposed of in this way the money box was passed round, the wassailers were given a little refreshment to help them on their way, and we went back to bed. I should perhaps mention one of these choir men who had a rather thin, high tenor, and who used to put in a kind of descant of his own to the chorus of "this jolly way-sa-il" every time it came in! John, this same tenor, also always put in a solo "Re-he-joice" in one hymn by way of 'improving' the three notes of the organ 'lead' for the choir. However there came a time - I suppose with advancing years - when he finally decided that he must give up his singing and asked us to "tell Mr Beacall as I'm leaving the choir 'cost I ca-ant sing". No doubt he would be sad to miss the annual 'choir outing', a great occasion every summer, usually taking the form of a trip to Weston-Super-Mare, though I think once they went to Stratford, with a sail along the Avon by way of extra excitement.

Another of my very early memories of Quedgeley was of visiting Miss Ia Robinson (Her full name was Maria, I suppose.) She was always very kind to us children and we used to go to see her on Sunday afternoons, when she would reward us with pennies in our 'Sunday pockets' (as she called them) after we had repeated to her any hymns that we had learnt. Only once do I remember her being vexed with me. That was when I had painstakingly learnt "All things bright and beautiful", which, as you may recall, has a chorus repeated after every verse. In the hymn book this had the word "etc" printed after most verses. I knew, for mother had told me, that this word meant "and other things". So when I came to the second chorus I carefully repeated, "All things bright and beautiful and other things" and Miss Ia thought I was being silly and rather rude!

I have very few memories of school, though I do remember one infant teacher who had only one arm. In order to sew she would pin the material to the top of the sleeve of the missing arm to hold it, and she always seemed to manage very well. In her day we used to march around the classroom chanting our tables to help us to learn therm. And once I remember feeling deeply mortified when I was sent to ask one of the little village boys how to do my sums!

The school house was attached to the school, and a door opening into it from our kitchen. The house had originally been three almshouses, I believe, and had none of what we should now consider basic amenities. We had to carry drinking water in buckets, usually from a tap at the head of the lane, though if this failed we had to walk about a quarter of a mile to a farm. To another farm we would go with a can for the milk, and could also buy eggs there, and buttermilk and skim-milk too if we wished.

Life was certainly hard in some ways, but on the whole, we were a healthy and happy family in Quedgeley School House all those years ago."

Marjorie Parsons (1907 to 2004)

On 10 October 2004 Quedgeley lost a very loyal servant, and I have put together a brief story of Marjorie's remarkable 97 years in Quedgeley.

It all really started when a young maid called Laura arrived from Reading with the new Rector for St James' Church. Laura took up her position at The Rectory and lived in. The Rector also employed other local staff and one maid happened to be Alice Parsons from the Bristol Road. Laura later married Alice's brother, James. In time James and Laura had three daughters called Phyllis, Olive and the youngest Marjorie. They were brought up in their grandparent's home, Pear Tree Cottage in Bristol Road, opposite The Plough Inn (now Friar Tucks). James worked in the Gloucester Docks, the timber yards and, in World War I, in the Ammunition Factory in Naas Lane in Quedgeley. The three girls went to the Victorian Church of England School situated in School Lane (where the fish and chip shop now stands). Marjorie told the local radio station some years ago that the school had two large rooms, two classes in one room and three in the other. The children stayed at the same school until they finished their education. There were many amusing stories told on the radio programme by local villagers, which I taped at the time and still have.

On Sundays the sisters went to St James' Church and sang in the choir and at certain times rang the hand bells and the bells in the Tower. Later, Marjorie and Olive were Sunday School teachers and the whole family made costumes for the Nativity plays which were held on The Rectory lawn in the summertime. As Marjorie grew up, she attended the Rector's confirmation lessons and joined the Girl's Friendly Society which was held in Quedgeley's first school room. This was built by the local squire in The Rectory garden and had room for about 10 people. It was demolished in the early sixties. In 1922 the Post Office next to the Plough Inn closed. Laura Parsons became the Quedgeley Postmistress and opened a new Post Office in her cottage opposite. Laura's husband, James, died in 1927. The first Village Hall was opened soon after on the present site and Marjorie enjoyed belonging to the Operatic & Dramatic Society and her mother helped her make many fine costumes for the actors. The Junior Imperial League met in the upstairs room at the Plough Inn and Marjorie also enjoyed their meetings and dances. Phyllis and Olive later married. Marjorie remained at home and worked for Western Trading in Southgate Street, Gloucester then at RAF Quedgeley during World War II. Living on the Bristol Road myself from 1936, I remember how busy the Post Office was during the War years. The Postmen would arrive on their bikes at 6:00am, sort the letters into rounds in the garden wooden shed at the side of the Post Office, then off they would go and stay out until the job was finished. Some readers may remember some of the Postmen and Postwomen: Mr Chew, Mr Uzzell, Mr Garrett, Mr Mansfield, Mr Charles, Mr Compton, Mr Stevens, Mr Ryder and Mrs I Bird. Laura Parsons ran the Post Office for 25 years and Marjorie followed on afterwards.

Figure 104 – Laura Parsons and postman Bill Compton

You walked up the long garden path with flowers around you and when you entered the Post Office a loud bell rang. The high wooden counter made it difficult to be seen if you were young. Laura died in 1947 and her daughter Marjorie, gave up her job at the Air Ministry and took over as Postmistress. It was long hours and sometimes she also went out delivering the post with her sister, Phyllis, who lived in Hardwicke with her husband Charlie. He would then have to run the Post Office and shop while they were out. Marjorie was Postmistress for 25 years, just like her mother, and retired in 1972 when the Post Office closed. Marjorie now had more time. She enjoyed many holidays with her sister, Olive, and brother-in-law, Lionel Bailey. There was time now to attend the Quedgeley Women's Institute evening meetings and the sisters enjoyed the outings. Marjorie became a Quedgeley Parish Councillor and her local knowledge was a great asset to the ever-growing parish. The Golden Age Club at the Village Hall was pleased when Marjorie joined. She soon got involved and later became the Treasurer. When Marjorie was in her nineties, she had an electric buggy and continued doing her shopping at Tesco. Her neighbours kept an eye on her, especially Noreen Smith. It was sad when she finally had to give up her cottage which she had lived in all her life. Her last two years were spent in Woolstrop House, where she was looked after very well. Marjorie still loved her local church but was now unable to attend. She continued with the Planned Giving until the last year of her life. I am grateful to Olive Bailey for helping me with the life of her sister. Olive lived to over 100 years of age in the Gloucester house that had been her home all her married life.

Myrtle Nash née Pready (1923 to 2018)

Myrtle was born on 4 October 1923 and died on 12 August 2018. She lived with her mother, father, brother and three sisters at Aston Cottage, near Rea Bridge, Elmore Lane, Quedgeley. They were a very respected family, who had lived there for many years. The family attended St James' Church and all the children walked to the school at the top of School Lane daily. People with money from the area built wooden bungalows along the banks of the canal and between the two Wars it was there that Myrtle and her sisters and brother learnt to swim. When Myrtle left school, she worked at Parkers in Gloucester, the well-known dry cleaners. George Nash arrived in Quedgeley and worked at The Air Ministry No. 3 Site near Aston Cottage, and Myrtle met up with him and finally married. They had two daughters, Elizabeth and Rosemary, then George was called up and served in the army. He had a tough time and finished his time in Korea. He returned home safely and Mark was born in 1954. George then worked at the gas works on the Bristol Road and later became unwell and died very young with a heart attack, leaving Myrtle a widow at 39 years old with three children to bring up. Myrtle didn't give up, she got herself a moped and went out working as a home help. Eventually she bought a small car. She also had many talents and started taking goods to sell on the Women's Institute Market Stall in Eastgate Street. She made cakes, jam, pickles, and grew and sold vegetables and flowers. It was a full-time job for many years and she became the Women's Institute Market Controller. Her son, Mark, and Myrtle loved cricket and enjoyed watching matches at Gloucester, Bristol and Cheltenham. Myrtle gave her time to Quedgeley. Myrtle was a bell ringer at St James' Church. She joined the Women's Institute in the 1950s and served on the committee and joined the drama group. She was a Parish Councillor. Her local knowledge was so helpful. Myrtle helped on many other groups in the community. We certainly miss her very much.

Revd Paul Dack (1925 to 2008)

The Revd F J Lanham, Rector of St James' Church (1947 to 1961), left to be priest-in-charge at Christchurch in Gloucester and the Revd Paul M Dack arrived from his parish in the Cotswolds to be our new Rector soon afterwards.

Revd Dack had served in the Army and had been taken prisoner in Burma. He did not talk about his time there. I expect it was best forgotten. He did tell us that this is where he made up his mind to take up the Ministry if he ever got home.

He first arrived one evening for dinner at our home at The Retreat Guest House in Quedgeley. I later took him to meet the St James' Church Parochial Church Council. He shortly took up his position, bringing his widowed mother, Florence, and her sister, Olive, to live with him. They were all well-received and soon settled in.

At the time, the Diocese had sold the nearby Headmaster's house in School Lane (which later became the first Quedgeley Parish Office) and also the land opposite The Rectory to build bungalows. Some of the money raised was used on The Rectory which was badly in need of updating after the two World Wars. Revd Dack organised the major works, which went on for months, and the family eventually had a modernised Rectory.

In 1957 Quedgeley was without a meeting place following the Village Hall fire. When Revd Dack arrived on the scene, he welcomed various groups to use The Rectory for their meetings.

Revd Dack set about clearing and planting the large garden with trees and flowering bushes. In the summer we enjoyed fêtes and parties there. The churchyard was also transformed, with curb stones removed and hedges sorted. He also gave the local Youth Club permission to use The Rectory Coach House for their meetings.

One of his first engagements was to attend the opening of the new Village Hall on 17 February 1962. It was a great day with the village pensioners invited to tea and the rest of the parish invited to a social evening. As Rector, he was automatically made a Trustee of the building and carried out his duties with pride.

Philip Parker of Quedgeley and I were both on the St James' Church Parochial

Church Council for the 20 years that Revd Dack was Rector. Philip was the St James' Church organist. Philip recently described Revd Dack as a true gentleman, very knowledgeable and with never a cross word to say. He was always willing to help people. I could not have put it better myself.

In 1982 the Diocese made it known that they wanted to amalgamate the church parishes of Hardwicke and Quedgeley. They would sell the Hardwicke vicarage and the Quedgeley Rectory and one of the clergy would have to leave. Revd Dack, being a Rector, could stay where he was for life but, being a gentleman, he said he would leave to allow the joining of the parishes. The two buildings were auctioned and my husband and I bought the Quedgeley Rectory and the Revd Geoffrey Stickland moved into the new smaller Rectory. It was built on the site of Quedgeley's first school, in the kitchen garden of the former Rectory.

Revd Dack went on to have many happy years working in and around Hasfield, Cheltenham and Leckhampton and we kept in touch by letter. I visited Paul in Nazareth House Nursing Home in Cheltenham just before his eighty-eighth birthday on 27 May 2013. He said he was enjoying life, with no washing nor cooking to do, and walked with me unaided inside the building.

It was a shock to hear that he had died there in August 2013. Paul had always said that he did not want a big funeral. I was pleased to hear that there was a Requiem Mass for him at St Peter's Church Leckhampton on 5 October 2013.

Kenneth Mansfield (1925 to 2008)

Quedgeley and Hardwicke residents were sad to hear that Ken Mansfield had passed away on 8 October 2008. The Mansfields had been in this area for a very long time.

Charles Mansfield was born in 1825. He married Ellen and one of their sons was named Thomas, born in 1858. Charles married a second time to Hanna. Over the years Charles had six daughters, five sons and three stepsons. He was an agricultural worker.

The 1881 Census tells us that the family was living on the Bristol Road, at Quedgeley. Thomas was now 23 years old, unmarried and a shoemaker. By the 1891 Census, Thomas was married to Maria. He was still a shoemaker living in the same area. He had a daughter and three sons. Thomas was a keen bell ringer at St James' Church, Quedgeley. His name can be seen on the board listing the ringers, inside the main door of the Church.

One of Thomas and Maria's sons was called Herbert. He was born 1889 and went on to marry Elsie in the 1920s. They lived at Manor Cottage in Naas Lane. Later they had Ken and his sister Vera, who were born there, and they attended the Church of England Infant School, which was on the site of our new Youth and Community

Centre in School Lane.

Herbert became the Clerk to Quedgeley Parish Council in 1932 and continued until his death in 1956. He worked during the day in his father's wooden shed. This was in the garden of his old home, opposite Friar Tucks, on Bristol Road. It was a popular meeting place. You were always made welcome and asked to sit on the wooden stool. The stove would be burning, and it was interesting watching the shoes being mended.

Ken did not follow in his father's trade. At 18 years old he joined the Navy, right in the middle of World War II. He served on HMS Orion. He was proud of the ship's exploits around the Mediterranean and on D-Day. He talked animatedly about his comrades and their tours of duty. Ken returned to Quedgeley after the War and met Barbara from Gloucester. They married in 1949. In the 1950s they were lucky to get a brand new flat at Parklands in School Lane. Their only son, Mark, was born there in 1956. The same year Ken took over being Quedgeley Parish Clerk from his father.

Ken joined the Hardwicke & District British Legion and gave them many years of unstinting service as a Branch Officer. He proudly carried the Standard, including on one memorable occasion at The Royal Albert Hall. He also enjoyed playing skittles for two teams, and was an active member of the local Labour Party.

Mansfield Mews, off Field Court Drive, was named to remember the well-known family. Ken and I served on the Quedgeley Parish Council together and I remember how his local knowledge was much appreciated in the ever-changing village. He will be remembered for his bicycle, scooter and Reliant three-wheeler that he travelled on to get to ICI Fibres for over 30 years. Barbara died in 1997 after a long and happy marriage.

By now their son, Mark, had moved from the area. He married Brenda and made Ken a very proud grandfather when Joel was born. Ken lived at his Parklands flat until ill-health forced him to go into The Knoll Nursing Home in Stroud Road, Gloucester. He was well cared for, until his death. The Hardwicke & District British Legion gave Ken a full Military Funeral on 21 October 2008. Revd Geoffrey Stickland carried out Ken's detailed instructions and we proudly celebrated his long and respected life. We will remember him.

Robert Brint (1926 to 2021)

Robert was the son of Charles and Lucy Brint and had a sister Kathleen. He died in Bath Road, Hardwicke, on 8 February 2021, aged 95. These are his recollections of his life in Quedgeley. They were written in his own words in about the year 2000.

"Uncles Sandy and George left school and went to work for Colonel John Curtis-Hayward the village squire who was then living at Manor Farm. Quedgeley House had been let, but the Curtis-Hayward sisters Isobel, Maggie and Evelyn lived there until their new house was completed. One of

George's duties was as coach boy on the family's horse carriage. The family would visit the Birchalls at Bowden Hall, the Darrells at Fretherne Court, Lloyd Bakers at Hardwicke and the Squires sister at Haresfield Court who had married Squire Robert Tidswell. George had to sit with his arms folded on the back of the carriage and upon reaching its destination he had to open the carriage door unfold the steps and help the ladies dismount. He was allowed to skate on the Moat near Quedgeley House sometimes watched by the Curtis-Hayward sisters. In those days it was possible to skate around the Moat which formed a square around a small central building (the shooting lodge). I would presume that the male members of the family shot wild duck in the winter there.

Uncle George would sometimes shoot in the shooting range which was a wooden building roughly where the Village Hall now stands; Uncle Ted Brint can remember playing there and tells me competitions were held there and there was a shooting League run in the area. George played in the Quedgeley rugby team who played their matches on the common, he broke his thigh whilst playing and when he came out of Gloucester Royal Infirmary his one leg was three inches shorter than the other so in effect he was disabled. When he was fit enough to start work again his options were limited and he decided to try his hand at basket making.

Mr Guilding (or Dr Guilding as he was known) owned the Plough Hotel (now Friar Tucks) and had decided to open a basket making business at the rear of the Hotel. Journeymen basket makers had been calling at the hotel on their journeys from the Worcester area to Somerset looking for work. These men were Mr Guilding's first employees and so basket making came to the village. Mr Guilding gave George a job and he was then trained as a basket maker. In 1908 he got his first experience of show displays when Mr Guilding entered baskets at the Show on the Oxleaze Gloucester which King Edward VII attended; the display was presented on the back of a hay wagon.

George married Hester Hanlon who was a dairymaid working for Mr Lovell at Highliffe Farm, his three sons Charles, Edward and Daniel will be remembered by some people. George had a family of eleven children over the next twenty-two years.

Mr Guilding sold The Plough Inn in 1911 giving George the chance to buy the basket making business and to transfer it. George who was living with his father in the thatched house approached his older brother Harry about setting up a business. Harry who was working for Mr Lovell at Highliffe Farm agreed to do so and so G. and H. Brint Basket Makers and Osier dealers was formed. The squire Colonel John gave permission for the business and buildings to be sited at The Thatch in front of Matalan as it is now (no planning permissions required). The business buildings, boiling vat and stock was transferred in two weeks, the members of the rugby team turned out en masse a couple of farmers sent their horse and carts and George's relations also turned out. Business flourished with contracts at Gloucester Market, hospitals and farmers in the area, war broke out and there was a glut of War Department work.

At this time no mains water, gas, electric was available as it was oil lamps and candles for lighting, cooking with the oven at the side of the fire, with a kettle or cauldron heated over the fire. In the washhouse or back kitchen would be a copper with fire under to boil water for baths, washing of clothes, and was used for wine making etc. Uncle Ted remembers when the pumps ran dry, he and his brothers along with Ernie and Bert Boulter would have to go over two fields to Acre Brook to get supplies.

The Great War came and the Munition Factory was built, Highcliffe Farm lost a lot of their land as did other farmers as far over as the railway line. Hawkes Bros supplied bread and cakes to the canteen twice a day, Ted helping when on holiday. He remembers when the workers started and finished work, mostly ladies, it was difficult to cross the road with cycles using them (we older people can remember the same thing happening when "7 Military District" evasion operation during and after World War II). He also remembers watching the steam engines and lorries drawing water from the brook between Quedgeley Lodge cottage and Mrs Scotford's house on the Bristol Road. This is roughly where the Cole Avenue complex of traffic lights are today, there were iron rails on the roadside and concrete steps leading down to the brook. He also remembers when Mr Browning was drowned at Rea Bridge when his taxi went into the canal. He was home from his service in Australia. George attended the inquest at The Plough, he was buried in Quedgeley churchyard, it was later thought that his grave was that of an Australian soldier, this was not true. The church bell was tolled to announce a death in the village and at the funeral the bell would be tolled for each year of his life.

Uncle George bought a second-hand gramophone with the big horn on top, his children plus friends Bill and Harold Cox, Bert Boulter and others spent much time listening to this new-fangled machine.

After the Great War, Quedgeley really began to alter from its rural nature. A football team was formed with a club house in front of what is now the Village Hall and the playing field was in front of Highcliffe Farm. Farms in the village consisted of Haywards, Rickards, Queen Anne Farm, Highcliffe, Manor Farm, Dawes Farm, Waterwells, Ashleys, Fieldcourt, Woolstrop, Green Farm, Quedgeley House Estate and Quedgeley Court. Mr Wixey began building in the Bristol Road, Naas Lane and Elmore Lane, joined later by his sons Fred and Cyril. Much of the munition factory land was still held by the government and pasture was rented out. Herbie Mansfield followed his father Tom as a shoe repairer. Mr Cale opened his basket shop, Hooper and Boulter and Mr Mills opened two garages, Jack Taylor (the school-mistress' son) opened an engineering works opposite The Plough; this was burnt down and he transferred the business to Gloucester and renamed it Llanthony Welding Co. The post office was run by Mrs Parsons and Margery, Mr Biggs opened a general store, Mr Newcome opened a baker with a delivery service, Miss Brewer opened a poultry farm, Hawkes baker and shop carried on as did George Brint's basket shop.

It was decided that a Village Hall was needed, George was prominent in fundraising etc. Mr Wixey built the Village Hall and it was opened in 1928. I remember it had a very high, long pitched roof built on walls perhaps ten feet high. The new school (which is where St. James Centre is now) was opened about the same time and the old school where the chip shop is now later became the cookery centre and carpentry room. Uncle Jim Brint remembers helping with the changeover.

Water, gas and electricity mains were now in position for people who could afford to change over to do so, it was many years before many people did. Telephones were very limited in their use in the village.

Captain Lodge built himself a house in Elmore Lane from a railway carriage, it was much admired inside and out. People came for miles to see it.

Living conditions at this time was very hard as the depression of the 1920s and 1930s continued. To claim unemployment pay, you were means tested. Mr Merrett walked from his cottage by the Plough to Eastington Park for many years where he was a gardener. Most villagers cultivated their gardens and allotments to put food on the table and kept poultry, some would keep pigs.

There was great rivalry as to who grew the best vegetables or who had the best poultry. Eggs during the glut period would be preserved in an earthenware utensil using Everglass. Mr Crowther, the coal man was the recognised slaughterman, he would come round to the house when called to despatch the animal. Pig meat would be given to relatives and friends, the sides of bacon would be salted and hung in the pantry for use through the winter when it had cured.

George and his brother used to keep three pigs and about 200 head of poultry, some in the Rector's paddock where St James Close Elderly Persons Home is situated. The breeds of poultry I remember were White Sussex, Rhode Island Reds, Indian Game, Black Leghorns, Wyandottes and Buff Orpingtons. When we lived further down the Bristol Road, our neighbour worked for a local farmer. One Christmas, the farmer's wife sent him home with some gruel for the children. It was in fact the water that the hams had been boiled in. His wife was furious and never forgot.

My father Charles had joined up with George in the business allowing George to follow his interest in achieving his work at exhibitions and shows throughout the country. His first priority with four other members of the Glo'shire Guild of Craftsmen was to get it back into a healthy organisation as it had declined sadly through the depression. They were successful as the healthy state of the Guild now shows. He won diplomas at the Paris International Show and London Shows, his work was exhibited all around Gloucester, Hereford and Worcester being presented along the way to the first Princess Royal (Queen Mary) and the Duke and Duchess of York (the Duke later became King George VI).

Charles followed on meeting the Queen at Badminton and closed the business in 1978. Their tools and memorabilia were displayed in a show case at the Basket Maker pub when it was opened and left on display. I am informed they have now been sold to an international collector and are in Hawaii.

My own earliest recollection is being carried onto the "Wave" and "Lapwing" which were passenger boats on the canal stopping at the bridges.

We moved again on the Bristol Road in 1930. I was taken ill and taken to Dr Colemans surgery in Gloucester. His waiting room was immediately cleared when they found I had diphtheria so I was then taken to Over Isolation Hospital to be joined by Mrs Myrtle Pready, (Myrtle Nash), Mr Bill Pready and Mrs Turner and we were all in the same ward. Myrtle tells me she was taken to the Gloucester Royal Infirmary by bus and put in a waiting room at the rear of the hospital, they cleared this waiting room when they found she had diphtheria and she was brought to Over. Myrtle remembers the beautiful flower in front of the veranda there and seeing her first long white enamel bath. All I remember is looking through a window at my grandmother with a bank of wild columbine behind her.

We all recovered and resumed our schooling. The headmaster was Mr Rintoul but he was often referred to as Captain Rintoul due to his World War I service. On the way to school along the Bristol Road we would play marbles along the gutter then as the whip and top season came in, we would whip our tops along the road to school at this time there were as many horses and carts as cars. Sunday nights the gates would have to be closed to prevent the cattle and sheep being driven to Gloucester Market from getting in and spoiling the garden. Mr John Stevens was then the Quedgeley Estate carpenter. When our pumps ran dry; along with other neighbours we would collect water from a deep well in the yard there. Mr Stephens died and he was taken by a bier pushed across Dawes Farm footpath. Uncle Jim Brint tells me about the same time Mr Harris of Dawes Farm was taken to his burial by horse and cart the same way. Quite a number of people would walk from their homes to get married at church. We were waiting to go into Sunday School at this time and an airship flew over (either the RT101 or R34). It crashed in France some months later, Later in the 1930s the Hindenburg Air Ship would come over at night with all its lights on.

On the way home from school one day Revd Hadow, the Rector, got off his cycle and summoned me over the road, telling me off for not touching my cap as he passed, he bid me attend voice test time at the Rectory. Several boys passed the test and we became probationer choirboys still sitting on benches in front of the choir stalls. Our rewards for singing in the choir was a summer trip to Weston or Bristol Zoo and to the Pantomime at Cheltenham with tea at the Cadena afterwards.

Mr Baldwin, the blacksmith, won £500 in the News of the World's crossword puzzle. The clue asked was a priest's coat, his answer of course was the only one correct, cape was the popular answer. The Smithy was covered in News of the World posters. We moved in the Forge Cottage in 1934 with Mr Webb still working the Smithy, he retired in 1937 when the Smithy closed.

The ground in front of the Forge, the Thatch and the Hawker used to be part of the common before the Enclosure Act. Records trace the Smithy being worked in the 1700s. When my great-grandfather moved into the Thatch in 1870, he was told by old villagers that the Forge was once a coaching stop designated by three poplar trees growing in front. He found three old tree stumps whilst helping his neighbour. He was told that years before, The Thatch was Venn's Farmhouse.

The Village Hall was used for socials (games and dancing for all ages). The Church Army gave slideshows, prizes for day and Sunday school, Sunday school parties, visiting concert parties gave shows and evening dances for adults. Mrs Hadow presented the Bethlehem Tableau, the cast would re-enact scenes from the Bible standing as statues; I was given the job of controlling one of the gas lamps in the audience area. The lights were high up in the ceiling with two cords attached to arms either side of the light, you pulled on the cords to either put the light out or on as required; usually these cords were tired to hooks on the wall.

At school on Empire Day we were lined up in front of the flagpole and then marched in front to salute the flag, the school tea party would be held at Quedgeley House courtesy of Mr Reginald Curtis-Hayward where tea and bun was distributed and races ran. The school playground in winter after frost used to get into an awful state, the school floors used to get covered in mud; it was in 1937 or 1938 that it was concreted over.

King George V Jubilee was a red-letter day in the village; the swings in the Recreation Ground were still a novelty having opened a month or so before. Captain Lodge brought a Band to the village, they marched from the Village Hall to the Church for a service and then settled down for the afternoon in the field opposite the Village Hall under the trees you can see today with mistletoe bunches growing. Sports was held in front of Highliffe Farm for all ages, we had a tea afterwards with the presentation of souvenir mugs. In the evening a dance was held for the adults and at dusk some kind of hot air balloons were released, one caught fire almost right away, the other sailed over two fields towards Robinswood Hill before it caught fire. The day ended with family and friends gathering at grandfather's cottage with the home-made wine following.

King George VI Coronation saw rain most of the day, there were a few races in the school playground and tea afterwards.

The hounds still met in the School Lane in front of Quedgeley House Lodge; they would either go on down the lane and avenue to a copse by Gadbury Cox's cottage called the Goss or down Naas Lane to Huntsgrove. Dick Brint and I got into serious trouble at home and at school when we set off to Huntsgrove and did not get back to school until 3:00pm. Milk was now being dispensed and we were given daps to do P.T. in. We were now old enough to start gardening classes, boys were paired up and given a small plot to cultivate in the school garden which was on the opposite side of the road to where the chip shop is and is now part of St James Close.

Carpentry and cookery classes were held in the old school.

Outside school we had the whole village including farms and the old munitions factory and footpaths to range over. Bluebells were picked in Carters Woods (Woolstrop) for elderly people in the village and home, cowslips picked anywhere dandelion heads were picked for the winemakers and blackberries and mushrooms grew in profusion on the munitions site fields.

Walks would be organised to Robinswood Hill across fields, there were a few houses when we crossed Tuffley Lane and on Stroud Road. Tuffley had not been built up then, we also walked to Haresfield Hill and Stonebench and riverbank. Cricket was placed at Fieldcourt Farm by the village team, we would go down to cricket practice and match days, once a year we were allowed to play in the marrieds v. singles fixture. Sometimes we would go to the Chapel for the Band of Hope and to concerts, there was also the Chapel outing in summer for the Chapel members.

The main attraction was bathing in the canal at the Boards; this was a piece of canal bank where the wooden piles had given way and allowed a shallow area of water to be used, it was about 500 yards towards Sharpness from Rea Bridge. Myrtle Nash was able to help me on my memories of this. Children would bathe in the water behind the Boards and the older ones would be taught and supervised by Reg Price (Taffy to all). He was a brilliant swimmer and could swim over the canal underwater. Taffy would stay with the learners until they could swim across the canal, once this was done under his supervision they could swim on their own. Jim Brint tells me, Taffy, him his brother and Muriel Webb would swim down to the Pilot bridge.

People would stop off at Mrs Pready's house to buy homemade ginger wine at a halfpenny a glass or two pence a bottle.

Through the summer we would also go round the farms to help with the haymaking and gathering sheaths of wheat building them into stooks for drying. The Bristol Road was now getting busy especially at holiday times and when cars from the north came through. As a result, quite a few houses became bed and breakfast establishments. It became a popular calling place for many travellers. The Plough Hotel became a stopping place for the Midland Red coaches travelling from Birmingham to Weston. Our Editor has information on the Birmingham connection to this. At the rear of the Plough was a café serving tea and refreshments and toilet facilities available. Coaches would fill the Plough's car park and I have seen them lined up on the Bristol Road to where the Tesco roundabout now stands. Several of us boys would be paid sixpence a day by Mrs Edwards to collect cups, wash up and keep the place tidy.

About 1937, work started on the building of No. 7 Maintenance Unit and big areas of where we roamed were fenced off.

Many houses have been lost from my boyhood, some of them are Mr Mills cottage and adjoining house, Waterwells Farmhouse opposite, two thatched cottages on the Bristol Road at the end of Naas Lane, Mr Mitchell's house opposite The Lawns, Mr Cale's cottage and bungalow, Dawes Farmhouse, Fieldcourt Farmhouse now partly utilised, Gadbury Cox's cottage at the Goss, Quedgeley House Lodge and its gardener's cottage, Woolstop Farmhouse, three cottages between Friar Tucks and the Thatch and Mrs Merrett's cottage behind them. Also lost were the cottages destroyed by the bombing in Elmore Lane, Miss Powell's house and Green Farmhouse, six cottages at the pitch where Cole Avenue complex is built and Quedgeley Court with Lodge and gardener's cottage."

John Phipps (1927 to 2008)

Late of Manor Farm, Quedgeley. We were all surprised to hear of the sudden death of John Phipps at Wycombe Hospital on 9 March 2008. As a friend to John and his late wife Sheila for over 50 years, I thought many readers might like me to write about these past residents of the parish.

Manor Farm is situated on the east side of the B4008 and has the Quedgeley bypass running through some of the fields. There is a large house situated in the middle of the farm. It is steeped in history and can be traced back to the twelfth century. That is a separate story.

In 1915 Manor Farm was taken over by the Government. Land was used to build a munition factory, where hundreds of local women filled brass shells for the War. The entrance was in Naas Lane off Bristol Road. The farmland was used to teach Ploughing and there was a 'Training School in Horticulture' for wounded ex-servicemen.

After World War I, Manor Farm was taken over by the County Council and divided into three farms, the tenants being Mr Phipps, Captain Clarke and Mr Hazel.

In 1937 the Air Ministry took more land to build No. 7 Maintenance Unit in Quedgeley. By this time there were only two tenants: the Phipps and the Brooks. The Manor House was divided into two homes.

Joseph Phipps and his wife had three sons. The eldest was William, then John (born in 1927) and Gerald who emigrated to Canada and has since died.

John went to Quedgeley Primary School from 1932 to 1939. He attended The Crypt Grammar School from 1939 to 1945 and was in National Service from 1945 to 1947 in the Royal Navy. Signalman Phipps enjoyed his time at HMS Raleigh and then aboard HMS Dunkirk.

After the Royal Navy he went to Veterinary College in London from 1947 to 1948. He hated London and decided to make his career farming and returned to Manor Farm.

The elderly parents retired and later died. William and John then took over running the farm.

In 1952, John met Sheila Gardner from Frampton-On-Severn and by 1954 they were married. They later had two daughters, Annie and Mary.

As the daughters grew up so Manor Farm came alive with young friends and relations. Hide and seek, cowboys and Indians, shooting walnuts off the tree with air rifles, pinching ripe apricots off the tree in the walled garden, catching frogs and pulling bull rushes from the ancient moat; they were truly wonderful times.

The family dinner table brought everyone together, not just the family but whosoever was visiting the farm at that time. Sheila was a bubbly lady and welcomed all to eat her delicious home-cooked food. One day she even had a patient from the Coney Hill Psychiatric Unit sitting at the kitchen table. He had gone on a walk-about and was lost.

John and his brother, William, worked together on the farm for many years. Many of the gadgets and pieces of machinery were designed and made by them: The Bale Sled, Grain Auger and Feed Mill, to name but a few. These were planned, cut, assembled and welded in the rooms that lay behind the 'Black–Door'. I am told it was like a cross between an untidy Blacksmith's Forge and a Pandora's Box inside. In the late 1960s William pulled out from farming and John was on his own.

If visitors turned up when John was working, he would invite them to have a go. When milking, he would say *"Now you have seen how it's done, have a go"* or *"Flip that Ram over, I want to give him a vaccination"*. The ram was usually 12 to 14 stone in weight. John would stand back and watch with his cigarette holder clenched between his teeth.

When the girls grew up, Sheila taught at the local primary school and will be remembered for her laughter and good humour. She joined the local Women's Institute. Later she went onto the committee and then did her time as President. John and Sheila would invite us up to Manor Farm in August, the month which had always been kept free from indoor meetings. John would put the hay bales out for us and we would each take along a picnic.

John hated petty bureaucracy in any form. When the 'Land Grabbers' moved in wanting to lay new water pipes and the Quedgeley bypass, he went to war – very successfully.

He also gave advice to many other farmers who found themselves entangled in a maze of paperwork. He went to court and represented many in the county. John later went on to write a book entitled 'Land Grab'.

Sheila loved acting and always took part in the many plays and pantomimes written by Ellen Parker for the Women's Institute or the Church. Mrs Dack, the Rector's mother, had us each week at The Rectory and we had hours of singing and acting. Because of her round figure, Sheila would enjoy being the fairy to make people laugh. Besides being a busy farmer's wife, Sheila also joined the St James' Church Parochial Church Council and later became a Churchwarden. She loved helping at the summer fêtes at The Rectory, Christmas bazaars and rummage sales in the Hall. All helped to keep the Church roof on.

Visitors were encouraged to join in discussions around the kitchen table and John was an exceptional listener. Topics ranged from 'How bad The Government had treated the Gurkhas' to 'Do we need a Parish Council?'.

He made people laugh with his dry tales. The vet came to the farm to drench some cattle and got crushed between a wall and a large steer. The steer was pushed away and the vet, winded, dropped to the floor. John said: *"Oi, don't lie around down there, I'm paying you by the hour mind"*. At a cheese stall at Gloucester Market, John said: *"How much is a pound of mouse trap?"* After the answer he said: *"Well how much is five pounds?"* A cheaper price was stated. *"Right then, I'll have two pounds off the five-pound block please; it'll be cheaper, won't it?"*

When the children were growing up, John only left the farm for a one-week holiday and one weekend break. He did also manage to attend his girls' graduation ceremonies. He did worry when Sheila went off to Nigeria to visit Annie when she was away on VSO. He told a friend: *"Last thing I need is a herd of cattle with Tsetse fly in exchange for those two"*. Annie is married to Rob and they live with their three children in Canada. Mary, Ken and family live in Amersham.

When Sheila died suddenly in 2001, John finally gave up his tenancy at Manor Farm and in 2002 moved to a bungalow off Sims Lane in Quedgeley, where he was very well looked after by 'his girls'.

The big builders moved onto Manor Farm and the new school was built near the Manor House. New homeowners are moving into Kingsway daily.

"The miracle is that life continues, the sorrow is that we do not". (Jane Walsh-Angland).

June Ryland (1933 to 2011)

June and I both started life beside the busy Bristol Road in Quedgeley. This was when we had no motorway, bypass or Severn Bridge to take the through traffic.

June lived at The Retreat with her parents, Mr & Mrs Richard Hooper. They shared the large house with June's uncle and aunt, Mr & Mrs Ernest Boulter and their son, Jon. I lived next door at Blenheim House with my parents, Mr & Mrs Herbert Ely and my sister Jennifer.

June and I went to the local Church of England Infants School. All the local children who lived north of the school went through the Recreation Ground, down the public footpath into the village allotments and ran quickly through the Woolstrop Farm field, where the cows grazed, then into the Rectory Lane, and finally arrived at the School where today we have the new Youth and Community Centre.

Our Mothers were great friends and got involved in all the village activities. They worked hard holding regular socials and auctions in the original Village Hall. They raised lots of money for Red Cross parcels, to send to the troops serving overseas.

We lived close to the Recreation Ground. It had three rusty swings, which were locked up on Sundays, a wooden bench, which had everyone's name carved on it and a huge oak tree, which the boys climbed. The field was always full of the local children playing.

Later, June went off to Denmark Road High School and I went to Ribston Hall High School. Neither of us went to college. We stayed very local and later worked for a few years in Gloucester.

Once we were both married and our children went off to school, we both followed in our parent's footsteps and got stuck in, to help out where we could in Quedgeley.

Over the years, we met weekly through Infant Welfare work, Women's Institute, Scouts, Parish Council, raising money to build the new Village Hall and the planning and building of the new Youth and Community Centre. We were both very involved with Quedgeley Community Trust, the Annual Show and Quedgeley News.

In the 75 years that I knew June and her extended family, we all had a very happy time working and socialising together, and I will certainly miss seeing her around.

Revd Geoffrey Stickland

In 1982 Geoffrey Stickland BSc (Hons), Dip. Theol. and his family moved from nearby Hardwicke vicarage and St Nicholas' Church. A new Rectory had been built in Quedgeley and Revd Stickland became Rector of the new United Benefice of Hardwicke, Quedgeley, Elmore and Longney.

Soon the Rector was seeking to expand the congregations of both Hardwicke and Quedgeley Churches. They had reached a total of 200 worshippers. Many new homes were being built each year.

We soon got used to the idea of seeing the Rector on his large motorbike. He also held a Heavy Goods Vehicle licence, which opened another chapter in our lives. Geoffrey Stickland made 14 return trips to Poland in 38-tonne lorries, together with church people following in their cars. They delivered thousands of parcels of food, clothes and medical supplies to churches and orphanages there. Each box of goods valued between £30 and £40. Finally, trips were made to Romania, Russia and Ukraine. Donations had been sent to Quedgeley from all over the country.

Cycling was another of his hobbies. The Rector and his wife went on tours with the Haresfield, Painswick and Quedgeley bell ringers. Geoffrey and Ruth also cycled 860 miles from Land's End to John O'Groats raising money for the Quedgeley bell fund. After that trip, they did what they called their 'side to side' trip from St David's in Wales across the country to Great Yarmouth. Another exhausting cycle ride they did was through Salamanca through central Spain to the shrine of St James in Santiago de Compostela.

Both Geoffrey and Ruth were keen bell ringers and Ruth was the Tower Captain of the team at St James' Church.

Abraham Rudall of Bell Lane in Gloucester made the original St James' Church bells. Quedgeley had six bells installed in 1732 with two more added in 1891 when they were last taken down for a clean-up. Enquiries were made in 1990 for a price to clean and retune all the bells. It was £13,000! It was decided to go ahead and the fundraising started straight away. Charities and foundations were approached, a flower and music festival held, local clubs written to, harvest auctions, coffee mornings, rummage sales, car boot sales, progressive ploughman's lunches were for sale, you name it, they did it. The largest amount raised was from Geoffrey and Ruth's Land's End to John O'Groats cycle ride which raised £2,000. The target was soon reached and the final bill of £13,800 was paid.

In April 1993, the eight bells were removed from the Tower with the help of 20 volunteers, saving a lot of money. The wooden frame holding the bells in place was rotten and was removed. A new steel frame was made to go into the upper tier which was mounted onto a new steel RSJ foundation. The eight bells were lined up outside the South Porch on the grass for the second time in 260 years. The next day they were collected and taken for refurbishment to Taylor's Bell Foundry in Loughborough. We thank the Rector and his wife for this because it was a task nobody else would have undertaken.

While Geoffrey was Rector, he also did a grand job of tidying up the churchyard, including removing curbs around graves to allow grass cutting.

We are most grateful for the three years he took touring war cemeteries in Europe getting information of the 25 soldiers from Quedgeley who made the ultimate sacrifice in the World Wars. Final information was found by Richard Graham (MP for Gloucester) through the Foreign Office. The list of the fallen starts on page 42.

Geoffrey and Ruth retired to Wales after 30 years at Hardwicke, Quedgeley, Elmore and Longney.

My Family

Herbert Ely and Sybil Doel were married in 1935 and their first home was called Blenheim on Bristol Road in Quedgeley. I was born there in 1936 and christened at St James' Church by the Revd H Hadow in 1937. My only sister, Jennifer, was born many years later in 1948.

World War II started in 1939 and my parents had evacuees from Birmingham living in the house with us. Dad built a concrete shelter, underground in the back garden. It had fixed benches and a wooden raised floor, because of the damp. There was an oil lamp hanging from the ceiling. It was cold in there but, armed with our gasmasks, we always felt very safe. My parents received the letter in Figure 105 (on page 132).

I WISH TO MARK, BY THIS PERSONAL MESSAGE, my appreciation of the service you have rendered to your Country in 1939.

In the early days of the War you opened your door to strangers who were in need of shelter, & offered to share your home with them.

I know that to this unselfish task you have sacrificed much of your own comfort, & that it could not have been achieved without the loyal co-operation of all in your household.

By your sympathy you have earned the gratitude of those to whom you have shown hospitality, & by your readiness to serve you have helped the State in a work of great value.

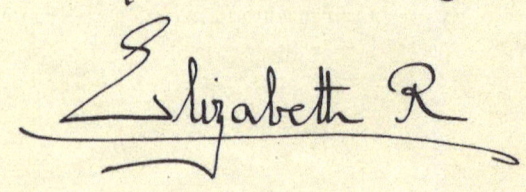

Elizabeth R

Mrs. Ely.

Figure 105 – Letter from The Queen Mother for taking in refugees

Chapter 6 – Our People

One field away from the back garden, Quedgeley's No. 7 Maintenance Unit, No. 3, Site was built. All the sheds were camouflaged in green and brown paint, but they still got bombed by the German planes. They also demolished a house in Elmore Lane, opposite No. 3 Site's main entrance. Thankfully nobody was killed. At home, we only suffered from a few cracked ceilings.

Dad went off at night with the local Home Guard, to watch for the enemy planes who followed the River Severn from the Bristol Channel, on their way to bomb the Midlands. It was still day light until 11:00pm and you could see the planes in the sky. When it got dark, the search lights on Robinswood Hill in Tuffley were looking out for them. Food was rationed, but we were lucky because both sets of grandparents were local farmers, with cattle, pigs, chickens, field rabbits and beehives.

Mr Hayward, a local Dairy Farmer, came round with his horse and cart in the mornings with a churn of milk and measuring jugs. We would hear him arrive and take our containers to the gate, to be filled. Mr Hawkes came with a horse and cart delivering his wonderful bread. He would be out all day and night travelling miles. He had lamps on his cart, which shone onto the ground, because everybody had to abide by the blackout rules. Hawkes Brothers had a bakery and a small grocery shop on the Bristol Road, opposite the Village Hall. Bennetts, the local coal merchants from Hempsted, delivered bags of coal with their lorry and carried the bags on their backs to our coal house. This was for the open grates, which heated our hot water. We also had paraffin delivered for the stoves. No central heating, washing machines and mod cons in those days.

My parents were involved with village life. Dad was a Trustee and a committee member of the Village Hall Committee for many years, and in the wartime was raising money for the soldiers and Red Cross. My mother helped with the Infant Welfare Clinic. She was a member of the Women's Institute and also the Mothers' Union. Later she served on the Parish Council. We were a church-going family and attended the local church services. I also went to Sunday School. Edith Fanner was the teacher for many years.

In 1941 I went to the Quedgeley Church of England School. I remember taking my Mickey Mouse mask and having to rest on a camp bed in the afternoons. The American soldiers were stationed locally in Quedgeley House, School Lane, and their big vehicles were up and down the lane, with the soldiers throwing sweets and chewing gum at the children and nylons to the young ladies.

By 1943, at seven years old, I travelled on Silvey's buses with six older local girls from the village to Ribston Hall High School, Maitland House, Gloucester.

In 1946 all the boys and girls received a note from King George VI regarding the end of World War II, see Figure 106 (on page 134) and Figure 107 (on page 135).

8th June, 1946

TO-DAY, AS WE CELEBRATE VICTORY, I send this personal message to you and all other boys and girls at school. For you have shared in the hardships and dangers of a total war and you have shared no less in the triumph of the Allied Nations.

I know you will always feel proud to belong to a country which was capable of such supreme effort; proud, too, of parents and elder brothers and sisters who by their courage, endurance and enterprise brought victory. May these qualities be yours as you grow up and join in the common effort to establish among the nations of the world unity and peace.

George R.I.

Figure 106 – Letter of gratitude from King George VI in 1946

Chapter 6 – Our People Page 135

IMPORTANT WAR DATES

1939
- SEP 1. Germany invaded Poland
- SEP 3. Great Britain and France declared war on Germany; the B.E.F. began to leave for France
- DEC 13. Battle of the River Plate

1940
- APR 9. Germany invaded Denmark and Norway
- MAY 10. Germany invaded the Low Countries
- JUNE 3. Evacuation from Dunkirk completed
- JUNE 8. British troops evacuated from Norway
- JUNE 11. Italy declared war on Great Britain
- JUNE 22. France capitulated
- JUNE 29. Germans occupied the Channel Isles
- AUG 8–OCT 31. German air offensive against Great Britain (Battle of Britain)
- OCT 28. Italy invaded Greece
- NOV 11–12. Successful attack on the Italian Fleet in Taranto Harbour.
- DEC 9–11. Italian invasion of Egypt defeated at the battle of Sidi Barrani

1941
- MAR 11. Lease-Lend Bill passed in U.S.A.
- MAR 28. Battle of Cape Matapan
- APR 6. Germany invaded Greece
- APR 12–DEC 9. The Siege of Tobruk
- MAY 20. Formal surrender of remnants of Italian Army in Abyssinia
- MAY 20–31. Battle of Crete
- MAY 27. German battleship *Bismarck* sunk
- JUNE 22. Germany invaded Russia
- AUG 12. Terms of the Atlantic Charter agreed
- NOV 18. British offensive launched in the Western Desert
- DEC 7. Japanese attacked Pearl Harbour
- DEC 8. Great Britain and United States of America declared war on Japan

1942
- FEB 15. Fall of Singapore
- APR 16. George Cross awarded to Malta
- OCT 23–NOV 4. German-Italian army defeated at El Alamein
- NOV 8. British and American forces landed in North Africa

1943
- JAN 31. The remnants of the 6th German Army surrendered at Stalingrad
- MAY Final victory over the U-Boats in the Atlantic
- MAY 13. Axis forces in Tunisia surrendered
- JULY 10. Allies invaded Sicily
- SEP 3. Allies invaded Italy
- SEP 8. Italy capitulated
- DEC 26. *Scharnhorst* sunk off North Cape

1944
- JAN 22. Allied troops landed at Anzio
- JUNE 4. Rome captured
- JUNE 6. Allies landed in Normandy
- JUNE 13. Flying-bomb (V.1) attack on Britain started
- JUNE Defeat of Japanese invasion of India
- AUG 25. Paris liberated
- SEP 3. Brussels liberated
- SEP 8. The first rocket-bomb (V.2) fell on England.
- SEP 17–26. The Battle of Arnhem
- OCT 20. The Americans re-landed in the Philippines

1945
- JAN 17. Warsaw liberated
- MAR 20. British recaptured Mandalay
- MAR 23. British crossed the Rhine
- APR 25. Opening of Conference of United Nations at San Francisco
- MAY 2. German forces in Italy surrendered
- MAY 3. Rangoon recaptured
- MAY 5. All the German forces in Holland, N.W. Germany and Denmark surrendered unconditionally
- MAY 9. Unconditional surrender of Germany to the Allies ratified in Berlin
- JUNE 10. Australian troops landed in Borneo
- AUG 6. First atomic bomb dropped on Hiroshima
- AUG 8. Russia declared war on Japan
- AUG 9. Second atomic bomb dropped on Nagasaki
- AUG 14. The Emperor of Japan broadcast the unconditional surrender of his country
- SEP 5. British forces re-entered Singapore

MY FAMILY'S WAR RECORD

Figure 107 – Useful World War II Dates Summary from King George VI

After the junior school, I went into the senior school next door to finish my school days. I was not a brilliant scholar and I wanted to be involved with art when I left school. I am still in contact with the old Ribston Hall girls now.

Boys and girls in the parish went to The Rectory in School Lane and Revd F J Lanham prepared us for confirmation. Finally, the Bishop of Gloucester would come to a Sunday Service at St James' Church and we would all get confirmed.

My father worked all his life at Fieldings & Platt, Southgate Street, Gloucester, and when I left school he made enquiries to get me a place in the Drawings Office. He was successful and I became a Drawing Office Tracer.

Leaving School was great. I joined the Quedgeley & District Youth Club. It covered all the Severnside villages and we had a great time once a week in the Hall. Harry Gage, a local showman, also put on a film show each week in the Hall, which was well-supported. I went along with Joan Winters, the Headmaster's daughter, to the monthly Women's Institute evenings. Both our mothers were members and they talked us into it and we were the youngest members there. I am still a member now. I became a member of the Gloucester Young Farmers Club held in Brunswick Road, Gloucester, and made many friends there, whom I still meet and go on holiday with. Gloucester Technical College ran domestic science and needlework courses and that was another night out. At an early age I became interested in politics and joined the Stroud Young Conservatives at Red Cross House Stroud, taking part in the social side and more serious debates, quizzes and public speaking contests.

In 1953 my parents decided to move down the Bristol Road a few houses to The Chantry (now a veterinary clinic), No 108 Bristol Road. In 1953 I met my husband Ken Meek from Elmore Back. In 1954 I changed my workplace and went on to The Telephone Managers Drawing Office at Bearland House, Gloucester and later became a Draughtman's Assistant. The same year Ken and I got engaged and then he had to do his National Service in the RAF. Two years later in 1956 we bought our first house, Sunnyside in Quedgeley, and the Revd F J Lanham married us at St James' Church. Ken then started working for R A Listers, Gloucester. I left work in 1959 to start a family, and we bought The Retreat Guest House, which catered for commercial travellers, visiting RAF Auditors, Moreton Valence Aerodrome staff and holiday tourists.

Our first son, Adrian, was born in 1960 and his brother Nicholas was born in 1963. Soon they were off to school and Ken started his own business, later called Gloster Generators Ltd, in Gloucester. That took off in a big way when the miners went on strike in the 1970s. With power cuts and three-day working weeks, the country suffered greatly. All the farmers wanted generators to be able to milk.

In the early years of our marriage, Ken was involved in restarting and managing the Quedgeley & District Youth Club with the late Peter Phelps. For 37 years, he served continuously on both Village Hall committees. That involved fundraising for the second Village Hall after the fire. Perhaps being a Quedgeley Parish Councillor was his most challenging role. I know it took a lot of his energy and time over the

24 years he gave to it. Over the years, Ken was chairman for a period on all three.

Anne Balchin came up with the idea of a new purpose-build Youth and Community Centre on the closed Church of England school site. A steering committee was formed and Ken served on it. The Centre was eventually built and has been a great asset to the local community.

For many years I served on the St James' Church Parochial Church Council and, like my mother, joined the local Mother's Union, Women's Institute, Infant Welfare Committee and Quedgeley Parish Council.

My husband and I both helped with the Women's Royal Voluntary Service 'Meals on Wheels' local service. The meals, cooked in our local school, were delivered to housebound residents by volunteers in the Severn Vale villages.

As mentioned earlier in my book, Quedgeley was included in the Stroud District. I was selected by the Conservatives to represent the new Ward of Quedgeley, Elmore and Longney. The election was held in June 1973 and I became the Councillor for the next six years.

In 1976 I received a letter from the Lord Chancellor, telling me I had been appointed a Justice of the Peace for the County of Gloucester. Quedgeley's Member of Parliament at that time was Anthony Kershaw and he had put my name forward. The County Magistrates and The Gloucester City Magistrates used to sit on different days, with their own clerks. Later they amalgamated and I then served at the Gloucester Magistrate Court and occasional at the Crown Court for 17 years. All Magistrates have to retire when they are 70. I enjoyed my work, which took me to serve in other courts in Gloucestershire. Many have now closed.

In turn, I was a Governor for Field Court Infant, Field Court Junior and Severn Vale Schools for many years and really found it very interesting. Later, Ken was also a Governor of the new Beech Green School in St James' road.

The Neighbourhood Watch Scheme was another of my interests for many years, attending meetings with the local Police and delivering leaflets.

In 1981 Laurence Sealey from Moreton Valence retired as County Councillor for the Gloucester Rural Area Ward No. 3, after serving it well for many years. I was invited to stand as the official Conservative Candidate, I won the seat and represented 16 Parishes in Severn Vale. This entailed going onto various County Council Committees. The greatest was being selected to serve on the South West Regional Health Authority. This covered visiting the hospitals in the area from Gloucestershire to The Isles of Scilly. These were very busy years, with everything else going on locally.

In 1982 my husband and I went to The Fleece Hotel in Gloucester and bought, by auction, The Old Rectory in Quedgeley which was being sold by the Gloucester Diocese. After a lot of work, we moved from The Retreat Guest House.

In 1983 Shirley Smith (from Elmore), Charles Herbert (from Hardwicke) and Ken Meek (from Quedgeley) were put up as Conservatives for the newly formed Quedgeley & Hardwicke Ward on the Stroud District Council. They all got elected. I left the Gloucestershire County Council in 1985 and joined the Quedgeley Parish Council in 1991. There were vacancies and I was co-opted on for three years. It was a busy time, dealing with the expanding population, but very interesting. I eventually decided it was time to retire and spend more time at home and in the garden.

The residents in Quedgeley were always after funds for the Church and other good causes. We held many house parties, coffee mornings and garden open days to help raise funds. In 1993 we started building a house in the front garden, No. 8 School Lane. When we moved in we let The Old Rectory as a Children's Nursery for several years. We eventually sold it for residential use in 2003.

In the following years, I have been caring for my immediate family and enjoying the company of my three local grandchildren. I attend St James' Church regularly and I have been a 'Friend of Gloucester Cathedral' from the time my two sons attended school there in the 1960s. I am a member of 'The Royal Society of St George' and 'The Gloucester Civic Trust'.

For 65 years I have served on the Quedgeley Conservative Branch Committee helping with elections and fundraising. I am also a Vice President of the Gloucester Conservative Association.

We enjoyed holidays with the family, boating on the River Avon, the Dorset coast and staying at our holiday home in Poole. Finally, motor cruising on the canal and river, between Sharpness and Evesham.

After 60 years of happy marriage, my husband Ken died and I sold No. 8 in 2017. I remain in Quedgeley, a short distance from where I was born.

I find time for Quedgeley Women's Institute (and have been a member for 70 years), gardening, playing bridge, painting pictures, researching my family tree and driving around visiting family and friends. I am now a proud great-grandmother to a little boy and a baby girl.

Appendix A – 1906 Quedgeley Parish Magazine

JANUARY, 1906.   1D.

Quedgeley Parish Magazine.

St. James' Church.

Rector: REV. STEPHEN CORNISH, M.A.

Churchwardens: COL. CURTIS HAYWARD, MR. H. LOVELL.

Organist: } MR. BEACALL.   *Clerk:* MR. S. KNIGHT.
School Master:

Assistant Mistresses: MRS. BEACALL, MISS S. STEPHENS, AND MISS SILVEY.

Sunday School Teachers: Miss Robinson, Miss Cornish, Miss Curtis-Hayward, Miss Nellie Harris, Miss M. Harris, Miss P. Brint.

Church Choir—Men: Messrs. Alfred Harris, Arthur Harris, T. Harris, H. Veal, W. Smith, W. Veal, J. Stephens, F. Townsend, and A. Webb.

Boys: R. Veal, S. Townsend, O. Rodway, H. Nash, Anthony Mansfield, Arthur Beacall, F. David, A. David, and A. Webb.

GLOUCESTER: H. OSBORNE, PRINTER, ST. MARY'S SQUARE.

Figure 108 – Church Magazine (January 1906)

Quedgeley Parish Magazine.

CHURCH CALENDAR.

Jan. 1. *Feast of the Circumcision.* New Year's Day. Holy Communion, 8.30 a.m.
,, 6. *Epiphany.* Holy Communion, 8.30 a.m.
,, 7. *1st Sunday after Epiphany.* Holy Communion at mid-day.
,, 8. School Re-opens.
,, 10. Evensong at 8 p.m.
,, 11. Band of Hope Entertainment, 7 p.m.
,, 14. *2nd Sunday after Epiphany.* Holy Communion at 8 a.m.
,, 17. Evensong at 8 p.m.
,, 18. Concert in the Schoolroom at 8 p.m.
,, 21. *3rd Sunday after Epiphany.* Holy Communion at mid-day.
,, 22. King's Accession, 1901.
,, 24. Evensong at 8 p.m.
,, 25. *Conversion of S. Paul.* Holy Communion, 8 a.m.
,, 28. *4th Sunday after Epiphany.* Holy Communion, 8 a.m.
,, 31. Evensong at 8 p.m.

Other Services at the usual hours.

We kept Christmas Day in bright sunny weather, and we trust the sunshine made its way into all hearts and homes in the Parish. The services were very well attended, and the number of communicants reached a high figure. The Anthem, "Let us now go even unto Bethlehem" *(Field)*, was well rendered, and with the Carols was repeated on the Sunday evening following. The collections amounted to £3 3s., and have been given, as in former years, to the Children's Hospital at Kingsholm.

The General Election is now close upon us. The following Prayer recommended for use by the Archbishop will, with the sanction of the Bishop of the Diocese, be said daily in Church until the Elections are concluded :—

Most gracious God, we most humbly beseech Thee, as for this kingdom in general, so especially at this time for all electors of members of Parliament that, remembering their vote to be a trust from Thee, they may faithfully and wisely make choice of fit persons to serve in the great council of the nation, to the advancement of Thy glory, the good of Thy Church, the safety, honour, and welfare of our Sovereign and his dominions; that all things may be so ordered and settled that peace and happiness, truth and justice, religion and piety may be established among us for all generations. These and all other necessaries, for them, for us, and Thy whole Church, we humbly beg in the Name and Mediation of Jesus Christ, our most Blessed Lord and Saviour. Amen.

SOCIETY FOR THE PROPAGATION OF THE GOSPEL.—The Rector has forwarded to the Ruri-decanal Treasurer, Mr. H. Allen Armitage, the sum of £8 18s. 2d., which is made up as follows: Church Collections, £4 12s. 7d.; Annual Subscriptions, £3 3s. 6d.; and by Boxes, 7s. 8½d.; also "Lent Savings," 14s. 4½d. This is exclusive of the "Special Whitsuntide Gift" to which a contribution of £1 12s. od. from this parish was sent per Mr. Zachary last June.

The Annual Prize-giving in connection with the Gloucester and District Sunday School Association took place in the Chapter House on Monday, Dec. 11th. We give the results as far as the country scholars are concerned. The Rural Dean, Canon Foster, was in the Chair, the speakers being Mr. J. W. Probyn and Rev. G. C. Keble. The former pleaded for earnest-minded men and women to volunteer for the work of Sunday School teaching, and reminded us how three most eminent men in their day, who all held the high office of Lord Chancellor, Lord Cairns, Lord Selborne, and Lord Hatherley, had regularly discharged this duty, and had found happiness in so doing.

Class III. (Age 10-11.) Prize: Arthur Beacall (Quedgeley), *Dean's 2nd Prize*. Certificates: Dorinda Summers (Morton Valence), Amy Taylor (Standish), Grace Farmer (Hardwicke), Lionel Clutterbuck (Morton Valence), Catharine Merrett (Hardwicke), Ethel Burford (Quedgeley).

Class II. (Age 12-13.) Prizes: Marjorie James (Standish) *Bishop's 2nd Prize*, Gladys Webb (Matson) *Archdeacon's Prize*, Elsie Barton (Morton Valence), Louisa Staite (Matson), Effie James (Standish), Doris Butt (Hardwicke), Daisy Langan (Upton St. Leonard's). Certificates: May Taylor (Standish), Mary Leach (Upton St. Leonard's), Leslie Clutterbuck (Morton Valence), Bessie Jordan (Upton St. Leonard's), Alan Beacall (Quedgeley), Annie Thurston (Upton St. Leonard's).

Class I. (Age 14-15.) Prizes: Ella Beard (Standish) *Bishop's 1st Prize*, Florence Barton (Morton Valence) *Dean's 1st Prize*, Alice Bullock (Standish), Mary Carter (Quedgeley). Certificates: Dorothy Carter (Quedgeley), Margaret Hogg (Hardwicke).

Owing to the sad death of little Christopher Cox on December 29th, the Band of Hope Entertainment which had been fixed for that evening did not take place. It will be given on Thursday, January 11th, in the Schoolroom at 7 p.m.

The concluding Empire Lecture was given on December 12th. The attendance was very small, which is a matter for regret, as Mr. Hobbs took Canada for his subject, and gave us a very interesting account of the growth and development of this great Dominion, in area equal to the continent of Europe, and full of natural resources. By numerous slides he illustrated the process of log-rolling, the work in the extensive corn districts, and life on the cattle and horse ranches, and the gold mines at Klondyke. As an instance of the care bestowed by the Government that settlers should be well provided with the means of education he showed how in the districts where land is allotted to emigrants, suitable plots are assigned at intervals for the erection of School Buildings. These Lectures have been given under the direction of the Victoria League, a non-party organization, which has taken upon itself the care of the graves of the Sons of the Empire who fought for England and died in the South African War.

We wish to draw attention to the Entertainment to be given by Mr. Douglas Lane and his company on Thursday, January 18th, at 8 p.m.: Front seats 1s., second seats 6d., admission 3d.

On Innocents' Day, after the usual service at 4 p.m., the children met in the Schoolroom for the Christmas Tree, at the same time prizes and awards were given for regular attendance at the Sunday School. The list this year is a long one, as the attendance has been unusually good. The following 14 have been present on every occasion:—Dorothy Smith, May Smith, Kathleen Smith, Bessie Townsend, Ada Smith, Alan Beacall, Arthur Beacall, Carey Carter, Harry Merrett, Dennis Mauler, Raymond Smith, Charles Townsend, Leonard Carter, and Willie Brint. The following 14 also have earned a reward:—Dorothy Carter, Mary Carter, Albert David, Frank David, Violet Vick, Kathleen Vick, May Pitts, Lily Pitts, Fanny Cale, Grace David, Ethel Burford, Sidney Townsend, Christopher Cox, and Hilda Crowther.

The Day School will re-open on Monday, January 8th. We learn with much pleasure from the *Citizen* of December 29th, that at the King's School, Gloucester, upon the results of the examination lately held for the election to a Monk Scholarship, value £8 per annum, for three years, the Headmaster has recommended for the Monk Scholarships Arthur Beacall (Quedgeley School); for a Pembroke Exhibition of five guineas, for three years, Charles H. Lovell (Quedgeley School).

EXTRACTS FROM THE PARISH REGISTERS FOR 1905.

BAPTISMS.

Jan.—Christine Cole.
Feb.—Lucretia Twinning.
Apr.—Frances Emma Townsend.
  „ —Charles George Brint.
  „ —Howard Goulding Luker.
June—Dorothy Pamela Scotford.
July—Gwendoline Nellie May Ryland.
  „ —Gertrude Eliza Langley Taylor.
Aug.—Ethel Amy Fanner.
Sept.—Elsie Mansfield.
Oct.—Olive Kathleen Parsons.
  „ —Violet Annie Parker.
  „ —Dorothy May Parker.
Nov.—Pamela Alice Scotford.
  „ —Arthur Job Mortimer.
Dec.—Minnie Kate Price.
  „ —Queenie Guilding (privately).

MARRIAGES.

Feb.—Charles William Cox and Beatrice Sterry.
Apr.—John Davis and Emily Louisa Smith.
June—Arthur Thomas Priday and Annie Louisa Weaver.
Sep.—Gerald Pomeroy Simonds and Marianne Cornish.
Dec.—Louis Woodman and Frances Elizabeth Cox.

BURIALS.

Jan.—Maurice Victor Chandler, aged 7 months.
  „ —Florence Julia Hanks, aged 1 year and 3 months.
  „ —Arthur George Mortimer, aged 1 year and 7 months.
Mar.—Charles Henry Browning, aged 79 years.
April—Eliza Sparrow, aged 81 years.
  „ —Caroline Davis, aged 47 years.
July—Gwendoline Nellie May Ryland, aged 1 month.
Oct.—Henry Merrett, aged 72 years.
Nov.—William Brown, aged 55 years.
Dec.—Sophia Sarah Seaton, aged 67 years.

Appendix B – Church Notes by Revd H Hadow

Quedgeley.

SOME HISTORICAL NOTES
CONCERNING THE
PARISH OF S. JAMES.

By H. E. HADOW.

Price - - - 6d.

All proceeds go to Church Funds.

Figure 109 – Revd Hadow's Notes

On the reverse of the front cover, it says:

"Dedicated to M. F. C-H whose enthusiasm inspired this humble effort"

QUEDGELEY.

The name of the Parish has been spelt in at least four different ways: and the earliest form appears to be "Quidzoy"—derived from the name of the stream called the "Qued" which runs periodically through the village. In 1137 Earl Milo—"Constable of Gloucester"—gave all the Tithes connected with the Church "as a perpetual thank-offering to Almighty God, S. Mary, and the Canons of Llanthony, Gloucester," and this settlement continued until the reign of Henry VIII., who dissolved the Monastery of Llanthony, and granted the Manor to Arthur Porter,* whose memorial Brass is to be found in the Church; and laid a royal charge upon the living, which has only been released in 1928 by being bought out by the Ecclesiastical Commissioners. A curious Law-suit arose in connection with Arthur Porter, over a dispute as to whether the occupant of "Field Court,"† which stands near the Church, should have the right to attend Quedgeley or Hardwicke Church. A very full account of the proceedings is to be found in "Gloucestershire Notes and Queries, No. 75," and it is worth noting that the dispute arose because one Richard Barrowe, who lived at Field Court, was accustomed to come to Quedgeley Church with his wife and family and servants to worship "in the Chappell of Our Lady" in the said Church; and while he was kneeling "at his prayers" one Nicholas Arnold, and "diverse other persons, did come, upon a certain Sunday in June; and by force and strength pulled the said Richard from his place"—which was regarded as the seat of Arthur Porter—and finally "did pluck him out of the Church by both ears"—while the said Arthur Porter "tide a dogge to his seet" that he

* Note.—*Inscription on Brass.* Nere this place lyeth buryed ye bodies of Fredeswid Porter and Mary Porter daughters to Arthur Porter Esquyer and Alys his Wyffe Ano MIVcxxxii on whose soules and all cristen Jhu have mercy ame.

† Note.—"Field Court" was inhabited by *Robert de la Felde* in the reign of Edward II. Possibly this is the origin of the name.

should not come back again. The case was tried in the "Court of the Star Chamber," in London; but the result of it seems to have been lost. It is a significant fact that this brawl in the Church took place "between 9.0 and 10.0 o'clock in the morning," when the Priest "was saying his office of Matyns," which he would have been doing before the Celebration of Holy Communion, as is the Church's rule to-day.

A fairly complete list of the Ministers, who officiated at Quedgeley, is to be found at the end of these Notes. The title of these Ministers is variously given as "Chaplain," "Vicar," and "Rector": and it is interesting to be able to record that at least two men, connected with Quedgeley, came to be Ordained—"William of Quedgeley," Sub-Deacon in 1283, Ordained Priest in 1290; and "John of Quedgeley," Ordained Deacon in 1319 and Priest in 1320, and appointed Minister to S. Bartholomew's Hospital (Gloucester).

In 1608 the Manor was bought by Sir William Dodington, who "built a convenient house for the Minister," and would have left the property to his son to succeed him—but "the son ran his mother through the body with a sword," and so could not inherit it. In 1666 a collection was made for the "lamentable Fire of London." In 1683 an Act was passed "that Quedgeley Rectory belongeth to the Right Hon. Talbot, Earl of Sussex."

There have been a great variety of Patrons of the Living, which until quite recently was a "donative"; which gave the Patron the right to nominate to the Living without the Bishop having to Institute the Incumbent. And amongst many names of the Patrons are found the Dukes of Manchester and the Earl of Warwick.

Some of the conditions under which the Incumbent lived have an interest of their own. At one time, he could claim 2 eggs from every hen in the Parish, and 3 eggs for every cock; the eggs to be collected on Good Friday, and presented on Easter Day: he could further claim 2 pence from every Communicant; one penny for every white cow; one penny for every barrel of cider; and a proportion of all apples and pears picked. In connection with this, a curious case is mentioned of one Vicar named Pierre Louis Bons, who charged a Mr. T. Hayward with having "two litters of pigs" and picking apples and pears, without payment. The bodies of Pierre Louis Bons and John Makepeace lie buried beneath the Altar in the Church. Another curious custom that existed was the right of the Incumbent to one calf if a man had 10; and if a man killed the fatted calf for his own use, the Incumbent could claim the left shoulder.

Amongst other incidents of historical interest may be mentioned the visit of Henry VIII. and Queen Anne Boleyn, who were met at Quedgeley by the Burghers of Gloucester; and tradition states that Queen Anne slept at "Read's Farm," which is now appropriately called "Queen Anne's Private Hotel." It also appears that a Bible seems to have been given to the Church on this occasion; though, if so, it seems to have disappeared. In 1549 land was given, the rent of which was "to repair the chalice for carrying Holy Water," for the yearly sum of 8d. Land had already been granted, the rent of which was to buy salt to make the Holy Water. In 1553 a man named Sheale was publicly excommunicated in the Church for "failing in his purgation." In 1563 the Parishioners were bidden to "buy a carpet for the Communion Table." In 1572 and 1662 an Episcopal Visitation took place, to which, amongst others, "School-masters" were summoned; and an Arch-episcopal Visitation is mentioned in 1576. In that year, 1576, Queen Elizabeth made a grant of land in Quedgeley to John Karnham, the rent of which was being used "to find a light burning on the Altar, and before the Image of S. James." The strip of land

Appendix B – Church Notes by Revd H Hadow

4

appears to have been called the "Lampe" land. What has happened to the Image of S. James is not recorded, but it is quite time that it was returned to its rightful place in the Church.

The Parish Registers, which date from 1559, are complete, with the exception of the years 1751-1812; and the Church Plate includes a silver Alms Dish, dated 1674, and a silver Chalice dated 1694; the latest addition being a beaten silver Paten made and presented in 1929 by an Art Student at Birmingham University.

The original Peal of 6 Bells were all cast in 1732, and bear the following quaint inscriptions: 1. "A. B. Rudhall cast us all"; 2. "Peace and good Neighbourhood"; 3. "Prosperity to this Parish"; 4. "Prosperity to the Church of England"; 5. "Thomas Hayward, Esq., and Thomas Vick, C.W., A.B."; Tenor. "I to the Church the living call and to the grave do summon all." Two additional Bells were added to the Peal in 1891. The Church was restored in 1857, when the North Aisle was built on, and the Organ Chamber and Vestry added; yet a great deal still remains to be done.

The List of Ministers, so far as has been traced, is as follows :—

Walter	- - 1210	C. Palmer	- - 1813
Adam	- - 1269	W. Foster	- - 1818
R. Archer	- - 1280	R. Jones	- - 1819
—. Walshe	- - 1329	C. Hardwick	- - 1822
—. Danyel	- - 1469	J. Lee	- - 1835
(Sir) Robert	- - 1493	J. Headlam	- - 1837
J. Evans	- - 1549	J. Russell	- - 1838
J. Bryan	- - 1552	T. Bowman	- - 1838
W. Gravestoke	- - 1565	E. Knollys	- - 1842
T. Wilcoxe	- - 1585	F. Alley	- - 1860
J. Jenyns	- - 1588	A. Bazett	- - 1862
J. Hurdman	- - 1650	A. Nash	- - 1876
G. Wall	- - 1662	E. Bryans	- - 1890
J. Makepeace	- - 1662	S. Cornish	- - 1896
T. Jowling	- - 1712	F. Grenside	- - 1907
P. Bons	- - 1713	E. Bartleet	- - 1917
—. Jauncey	- - 1770	H. Hadow	- - 1925
J. Forthlock	- - 1777	G. Harvey	- - 1941

Appendix C – 1861 Census (as printed)

QUEDGELEY is a village and parish, 3 miles south from Gloucester Station, 9 from Stroud, and 12 from Cheltenham, in the eastern division of the county, Whitstone and Dudstone hundreds. The Gloucester Union and County Court district. Gloucester Rural Deanery and Archdeaconry, and Gloucester and Bristol Diocese: It is situated on the high road from Gloucester to Bristol. The Church of St James is an old stone building in the Decorated or Middle Pointed style; it has been repaired, and has spire, tower with six bells and clock, nave, aisles, porch and chancel. The register dates from the year 1577. The living is a Rectory, yearly value £185, with residence and 2 acres of glebe land, in the gift of J. Curtis-Hayward Esq. and held by the Revd Alfred Young Bazett, MA., of Trinity College, Cambridge. There is a National School for children in the parish. £1 is annually distributed among the poor. Quedgeley House is a handsome mansion, pleasantly situated in a fine park; it is the seat of John Curtis-Hayward, Esq. J.P. who is lord of the manor and chief landowner. The chief crops are wheat, beans, potatoes, roots and pasturage. The soil is blue lias; subsoil, various. The area is 1,453 acres, and the population in 1851 was 401; gross estimated rental. £5,292; rateable value £4,525.

Quedgeley tithing has a population of 344, and Woolstrop hamlet a population of 57.

PARISH CLERK David James. POST OFFICE David James, postmaster.

Letters arrive from Gloucester 8-40 a.m.; dispatched at 6pm.

The nearest money order office is at Gloucester.

NATIONAL SCHOOL Miss Jane Gander, mistress.

Private Residents
Bazett Revd Alfred Young, M.A. Rectory

Curtis-Hayward John, esq. J.P. Quedgeley House

Waddy, Mr Henry

Commercial
Baker Henry, farmer, Manor Farm.

Bick John, beer retailer & boot & shoe maker

Browning Ralph John, farmer

Cole Thomas, carpenter & wheelwright

Fawkes Morris, farmer, Netheridge Farm

Golding Thomas, farmer

Harris Charles, carpenter

Hawkes John, Yeoman

Hawkes Saml. & Edward, bakers & shop keepers

James David, carpenter

Jenner Thomas, baker & shopkeeper

Jones Daniel, farmer

Kembery John, farmer, Waterwells Farm

Merrett Henry, farmer, Quedgeley Farm

Priday Sarah (Mrs) beer retailer

Smith Thomas, farmer

Taylor Daniel, blacksmith

Welling William, tailor

Looking through the censuses which follow 1861, I was amazed how many times the Clergy, Postmasters, Parish Clerks, Masters and Mistresses were replaced. The spelling of resident's names also changed every 10 years. You will notice that all the names of the people who were living in Quedgeley in 1861, are not included in the census. At that time 401 parishioners lived in 80 homes, average of 5 per household.

Index

We have used groups to help you navigate the index: Buildings, Businesses, Churches (includes Clergy), Clubs, Estates, Legal, Locations, Organisations (includes Schools), People, Roads, Royalty, Waterways and finally World Wars.

B

Buildings

Forge Cottage	6
Health Centre	80
Indian Bungalow	8
Library	79
Packers Cottage	6
Police Station	80
Riversmead Farm	8
St James Centre	75, 85
The Chantry Animal Pound	4
The Rectory	48
The Retreat Guest House	17
Village Hall	20, 70
Youth and Community Centre	75

Businesses

Basket Makers	110
Daystrom	5
Friar Tucks	See The Boat Inn
Hawkes' Bakery	4
Jowett's Grocery	4
Quedgeley News Limited	108
Quedgeley Social Club Limited	76
Queen Anne Farm	See The Thatch Restaurant
Read's Farm	See The Thatch Restaurant
Severnvale Shopping Centre	77
Tesco	77, 79
The Basket Maker	See The Haywain
The Boat Inn	15
The Haywain	78
The Little Thatch	See The Thatch Restaurant
The Plough Hotel	See The Boat Inn
The Thatch Inn	See The Thatch Restaurant
The Thatch Restaurant	6

C

Churches
  Clergy
    Past Church Ministers 45
    Revd Dack, Paul 71, 118
    Revd Hadow, Herbert 48
    Revd Hayward, Winstone 37
    Revd Lanham, Frederick 20, 51, 64, 118, 136
    Revd Makepeace, John 33
    Revd Stickland, Geoffrey 130
  Methodist Church 4, 81
  St James' Church 8, 33
    Churchyard 40
    Marriage Register (1559-1836) 46

Clubs
  Brownies 95
  Cricket Team 18
  Cubs 95
  Football Team 18
  Golden Age 99
  Mothers' Union 89
  Rainbows 95
  Scouts 95
  Women's Institute 90
  Youth Club 92

E

Estates
  Field Court Estate 8, 59
  Netheridge Estate 4, 60
  Quedgeley Court 5
    Lodge 5
  Quedgeley House Estate .... *See* Woolstrop Manor
  The Manor 53
    Manor Farm House 6
  Woolstrop Manor 54
    Woolstrop Farm 58

L

Legal
- Enclosure Acts of 1841 and 1866 4
- Gloucester Poor Law Union 14

Locations
- Brookthorpe 8
- Caer-Glow .... *See* Glevum
- Dudstone Kings Barton Hundred 7
- Elmore Back 136
- Glevum 13, 14
- Hardwicke 5, 13, 28
- Hempsted 5, 11, 13, 60, 133
- Kingsholm 13
- Saul 17
- Stonebench 9, 32
- Stonehouse 5
- Whitstone Hundred 7
- Woolstrop Hamlet 7

O

Organisations
- Infant Welfare Clinic 97
- National Filling Factory No. 5 .... 9, 60
- Parish Council .... *See* Town Council
- Quedgeley Community Trust 108
- Quedgeley Village Trust 108
- RAF Maintenance Unit 9, 62
- RAF Quedgeley .... *See* RAF Maintenance Unit
- Schools 82
  - Beacall T 82, 101
  - Blake, Gordon 86
  - Chislett 87
  - Comprehensive School .... *See* Severn Vale County Secondary Modern School
  - Cox, Valerie 85
  - Field Court Schools 87
  - Lutkins, Tony 86
  - Mortimore, Anne 87
  - Robertson, Mona 85
  - Severn Vale County Secondary Modern School 86
  - Spiers, Leonard 86

Stokes, David 87
The Church of England School 83
The Early Schools 82
The National School 82
The Victorian School .... *See* The National School
Townsend, Roy 85
Winters, Fred 85
Town Council 100

P

People
Balchin, Anne 75, 76, 108, 137
Beacall, Mary 112
Beacall, T 82, 101
Blake, Gordon 86
Brint, Elaine 20
Brint, Robert 120
Cale Family 110
Carter, Cary 43, 58
Chislett 87
Cole, John 59
Coventry, Flight Lieutenant Robert 62
Curtis-Hayward Family 18, 34, 53, 55, 59, 60, 70, 82, 108, 109
Darrell, Sir Lionel 70
Dean, Albert and Pat 79
Edwards, John Ivor 15
Ely, Herbert 21, 71, 131
Ely, Jennifer 20, 85
Ely, Sybil 21, 97, 98, 100, 131
Gage, Harry 21
Gardner, Ivy 17
Gardner, William 17
Gaskin, Group Captain Peter 66, 67
Gleed, Ken 67
Hall, Jacqueline .... i, 108
Hill, Group Captain Ted 67
Hinder, Mary 76, 99
Kyle, Air Vice Marshall Richard 67
Lutkins, Tony 86
Macloud, Marion 19
Mansfield, Kenneth 119
Mayo, Cyril 71, 105

Meadows, Lucy	49
Meek, Caroline	28, 64, 92, 98, 108
Meek, Kenneth	21, 25, 64, 71, 93, 105, 136, 138
Mortimore, Anne	87
My Family	131
Myatt, Alan	87
Nash, Gilbert	17
Nash, Myrtle	117
Nicholas, Cllr Roy	77
Norman, Ursula (Sue)	28, 99
Oakes, William (Bill)	30, 80
Parker, Philip	95, 106, 118
Parsons, Marjorie	115
Phelps, Peter	93, 136
Phipps, John	126
Ploutarchou, Flying Officer Lynne	67
Pready, Myrtle	*See* Nash, Myrtle
Roach, J	17
Robertson, Mona	85
Ryland, June	92, 98, 108, 129
Sandover, WPC Marion	61
Saxons	
Anglo-Saxons	14
Chief Cwoed	14
Spiers, Leonard	86
Stokes, David	87
Stroud, Graham (Tony)	21, 64, 100, 108
Stroud, Nancy	64, 95, 98
Tudor, Kevin	108
Turner, Jean	108
Winters, Fred	85
Wixey, George	70, 71

R

Roads
Bristol Road	4
Church Drive	13
Cole Avenue	5, 126
Crockens Lane	*See* Sims Lane
Davillian Court	8
Elmore Lane	8
Gloucester Ring Road	5

Goodridge Avenue	5
Kings Way	*See* Bristol Road
Longney Lane	*See* School Lane
Naas Lane	8, 14
School Lane	8
Sims Lane	7, 8
Woolstrop Way	8

Royalty

Dukes of Gloucester	32
H.R.H. Prince of Wales	32
King Henry VIII	31
Princess Margaret Rose	32
Princess Mary Tudor	30
Queen Anne Boleyn	31
Queen Elizabeth I	31
Queen Elizabeth II	32
Queen Mary	32
Royal Visitors	30

W

Waterways

Bristol Channel	9, 10
Canal	*See* Gloucester & Sharpness Canal
Dimor Brook	4
Gloucester & Berkeley Canal	*See* Gloucester & Sharpness Canal
Gloucester & Sharpness Canal	4, 5, 7, 8, 11, 17
Plynlimon	9
Qued Brook	4
River Severn	8, 9
Sabrina	14
Waterways	4, 9

World Wars

War Memorial	42
World War I Roll of Honour	42
World War II Roll of Honour	44

Printed in Great Britain
by Amazon